JONATHAN EDWARDS

THE NARRATIVE OF A PURITAN MIND

Riverside Studies in Literature

Riverside Studies in Literature

GENERAL EDITOR · GORDON N. RAY

Jonathan Edwards

The Narrative of a Puritan Mind

EDWARD H. DAVIDSON

University of Illinois

HOUGHTON MIFFLIN COMPANY • BOSTON

CONTENTS

INTRODUCTION

THE NARRATIVE of Jonathan Edwards is interesting not for the details of his biography nor for the impact he made on his age, but for the drama of the man's mind as it faced, struggled against, and rejected the major ideas of his time. This study is, therefore, an intellectual biography of a man who lived through the central issues of the latter part of the seventeenth and the first half of the eighteenth century and who made those issues the structure of his own life and mind. Edwards confronted the eighteenth-century dilemma — how does one know what he thinks he knows? — and made it into a cardinal principle of belief: what one knows depends on what he apprehends of God and His world. More importantly, Edwards assumed that this dilemma was one of single, private consciousness: how one lives is most probably dependent on what he believes. If he is sensitive to everything that makes up living — the air that blows, the sky that changes its contour and color every hour, and the varieties of his own moods — then he is likely to see that belief and religious faith are not abstractions located in the mind but that ideas have body, tissue, living strength. Edwards felt with the intensity of exceptional desire yearning for wonder in the commonest details of life. He wrote in prose because he was a clergyman intended by God to find that small particle of truth which God allows man to know; yet he had the exquisite sensitivity of a poet.

Thus in Edwards converged the two master designs of his age — one, the Puritan conviction that man lives a parlous life in a world ruined by centuries of Satan's craft and man's unfeeling abandonment of God, yet lives with his senses and his mind awake to the grace which God holds out betimes even to the chief of sinners; the other, the rationalist-empirical heritage, quite new it was, which derived from Bacon and was invigorated by Newton and Locke. In this new thought Edwards gained his first guiding ideas of substance: every atom is part of an infinite design which all together has meaning and purpose; in the intensity of feeling from the ends of one's fingertips to the top of one's mind, a man can learn all he need know of himself and of his God. What the Puritan had long known as "the second book" (the first being, of course, the Bible), Edwards raised to an importance in men's daily lives nearly equal to that of Holy Writ. The world, like the Word, had meaning, and it could be found if man but looked.

The meeting and confluence of two modes of thought, so disparate they seem at first view, often effect a kind of baroquerie of the mind. In Edwards's own day, in the distant lands of Europe he never saw, the joining of the Renaissance idea of form and the daring imagination of man's mind produced the fantastic exuberance of baroque painting; and that master of all composers, Johann Sebastian Bach, who was nearly Edwards's contemporary, brought to an ultimate peak the medieval Catholic and the sterner Protestant in the organ preludes and the St. Matthew Passion. These moments of dazzling consummation of styles nearly exhausted, as though in their final expression they achieve a sacred vitality, haunt the imaginations of men because the end of a style or a system of thought is supposed to mean the end of its expression. It is not always so: genius may flower even when a master principle has been declared dead. In this respect Edwards can well be called "a Puritan baroque": though his style could be as chill and neat as that admired in the age of Dryden, his imagination was all compact of wonder, exuberance, and joy. And though his logic was not as tempered as the reasonings of Schoolmen, his mind worked to break that logic and to find, even in its precepts which seem to mark an end of thought, a new way to adventures of the mind. Though he lacked an academy, or even any first-rate mind as good as his own on which to hone it, Edwards had the good fortune to live at the summit of two systems of thought, two modes of looking at man and the universe, two methods of inquiry into the meaning of one's self. He lived in both and he used both, sometimes separately, sometimes together. That inconsistencies should arise was inevitable; yet they were the incentives to new directions his mind took, for it was a mind which never closed.

Yet if Edwards, as a lonely man and as a Puritan theologian, conducted a personal, a spiritual journey through the intellectual problems of the eighteenth century, he was, despite his remoteness from the swirl of fashion and the seethe of opinion, as much, and as significantly, a spokesman for his time as were, in their quite differing ways, Voltaire and Dr. Johnson. Edward's pilgrimage of the mind was through those pathways of rationalist and empirical logic under which virtually all thought of his age was subsumed. Yet, even as he was of his age, he was apart from it: rather than discover the balanced, commonsensical, modest, and demonstrable conclusions which so many in the century found appeasing to the nudgings of their minds and consciences, Edwards saw that behind the bland façade, the ordered system, and the appropriate distance between a beneficent God and His children on earth was the dark terror of the human spirit, still as distressed, still as despairing as it had ever been.

The striking quality of Edwards's spiritual pilgrimage was that it was like that of Pascal a century earlier or of Kierkegaard a century later: it was a journey through the dark night of the soul when the whole world of thought and of religion had become convinced that all such darkness and despair had disappeared in the clear light of human reason. It was a pilgrimage through the eighteenth-century dilemma of consciousness when, for all respectable purposes, that dilemma had gone the way of such absurdities as witchcraft, the philosopher's stone, and the primitive bestiality of man. In our day these minds, so brilliant and yet so misplaced in their world and time (but where else would they have been comfortable?), offer themselves with special cogency, even in tone and fashion. They — Pascal, Edwards, Kierkegaard — have already, we say, acted out and passed through our own condition of consciousness. Yet it must be declared at once and very clearly: Edwards was not doing for us what we should like to have done and cannot do for ourselves. Edwards was of his age, not of ours; and even if the rigorous demands of hard thinking and a tough-minded search for God have returned to plague and to enlighten us as they did Edwards, we must be accurate in all our surmises and try to see them as Edwards saw them.

Edwards dared to seek the deeper psychology (the phrase is Henry James's applied to Hawthorne) when the data of introspection and the clues to self-understanding were presumably all located, not in the single being, but in the outside world of sense data. He returned to the full and awful logic of the Covenant in a day when the terms of the Covenant had been so revised that the codicils were all in man's favor and God could but benignly acquiesce. He did so, not because he wished to bring to his countrymen the dire terror of God's vengeful justice but because he knew that the Covenant was the Puritan's or any man's firmest awareness of the truth as against what he called "the ghastly hold of reality." He launched a brilliant assault on the illusion that man has a free will, not because he wished to belittle man in the awesome splendor of God but because he tried to turn men inward and upon their own consciences where truth is never easy and where pain ever lurks. He ventured to raise not only the eighteenth-century question — How does a man know what he thinks he knows? — but also the problem which seventeenth-century Puritanism had posed — What shall a man become in order to be saved? In his life and writings he offered an apologia not only for himself but for his age. The record is there for us to read and interpret along the way of Edwards's lifetime journey.

*   *   *   *   *

I am greatly indebted to all those who in recent years have studied Edwards and have made his writings a primary text in the understanding of American thought and writing. Many of these critics and commentators are cited in the Notes; the rest are a silent but necessary part of this narrative.

The editors of the *Journal of the History of Ideas* have permitted me to reprint portions of my article "From Locke to Edwards," which first appeared in that quarterly.

To the librarians of several universities I owe much in the way of favors and scholarly assistance. The officers and staff of the Widener and Houghton Libraries were most gracious throughout my year's residence as a visitor at Harvard University. Miss Isabelle Grant and Miss Eva Faye Benton of the Library of the University of Illinois offered invaluable aid. To the Research Board of the Graduate College of the University of Illinois I am most grateful for financial assistance and generous grants-in-aid. I acknowledge that my colleagues in the English department of the University of Illinois have provided a true concord of minds.

AN EDWARDS CHRONOLOGY

1703   Edwards born October 5 at East Windsor, Connecticut.

1715   Wrote "Of Insects" and "Notes on Natural Science."

1716   Entered Yale College, where he spent four years as an undergraduate and two as a student of theology.

1722   Went in August as minister to a Presbyterian church in New York City, where he remained eight months.

1723   Left New York in April; spent the summer in East Windsor.

1724   Elected a tutor at Yale; his teaching interrupted by illness in 1725; resigned the tutorship in 1726.

1727   Elected assistant minister to his grandfather, the Reverend Solomon Stoddard, minister of the church in Northampton, Massachusetts. Married Sarah Pierrepont in July.

1729   Death of Stoddard in February.

1731   Invited to preach in Boston; delivered *God Glorified in Man's Dependence*, published in that year.

1735   Beginning of the first phase of the Great Awakening.

1737   Decline of the Awakening. *A Faithful Narrative of the Surprising Works of God in the Conversion of Many Hundred Souls.*

1740   Revival of the Awakening. Edwards joined briefly by George Whitefield in the ministry of conversion.

1741   *Personal Narrative* written. *The Distinguishing Marks of a Work of the Spirit of God* published.

1742   End of the Awakening. *Some Thoughts concerning the Present Revival of Religion in New England.*

1746   *A Treatise concerning Religious Affections.*

1747   Death of the Reverend David Brainerd, engaged to Edwards's daughter Jerusha, in October.

1748   Beginning of the dissension in Edwards's church.

1749   *An Account of the Life of the Late Reverend Mr. David Brainerd.*

1750   Preached the Farewell Sermon, July 1.

1751   Settled in Stockbridge, Massachusetts, as minister of the church and missionary to the Indians.

1754   *Freedom of the Will.*

1755   *The Nature of True Virtue* and *Concerning the End for Which God Created the World* written; published 1756 as *Two Dissertations.*

1757   Named President of Princeton College.

1758   Assumed office in January; died of smallpox March 22; buried in Princeton. *The Great Christian Doctrine of Original Sin Defended.*

JONATHAN EDWARDS

THE NARRATIVE OF A PURITAN MIND

1

The Inclining World of God

THE beginnings of Jonathan Edwards are so typical of New England clergymen of the eighteenth century that the opening narrative of his life reads like an oft-told tale. He was of the fourth generation of Edwardses in Connecticut and was the second in the family line to be a minister (the other two Edwardses, grandfather and great-grandfather, were prosperous in the ways of trade and in the ownership of land). His great-great-grandfather Richard, the first Edwards of whom any record survives, lived and died in England; he had gone to St. John's College, Oxford, and, if the records are correct, could sign himself B.A. and M.A. William Edwards, the next in line, was a cooper who came to Connecticut about 1635 and resided in Hartford. His second son, named Richard for his paternal grandfather, was born in Hartford in 1647 and lived there all his lifetime of seventy-one years, during which he contrived to acquire a considerable competence of this world's goods both in his trade and in his merchandising; at his death in 1718 his estate was valued at twelve thousand pounds. His life was not, however, a smooth and gracious one: his wife, Elizabeth Tuttle, who bore him six children, showed signs of an unsound mind. Throughout twenty-four years of marriage Richard bore his travail decently and quietly; then, on an occasion almost unprecedented in New England annals, he brought an action for divorce which in October, 1691, was granted on Scriptural grounds. A year later he married Mary Talcott, daughter of an early settler of Hartford, and lived the remainder of his life in dignity and forbearance of his critics. The divorce action may be regarded as prophetic of the after-history of the Edwardses: it marked a sturdy self-reliance that reappeared in the sons and grandsons of the eighteenth century, an almost irascible devotion to a single-purposed cause in one's life, and an unwillingness to yield to the advice of common sense and to the normal proprieties of life. Jonathan, the grandson, would face his detractors in Northampton and, though finally beaten, never waver in his devotion to the cause he believed just and God-ordained; and the insanity (if one trusts the suggestions of family

1

inheritance and taint) may have had its later effects in Jonathan's
son Pierrepont, whose life was both drunken and incompetent,
and in a famous grandson, Aaron Burr, who tried to unseat a new
government. Insanity and genius may not be far apart in a family
which achieves distinction and knows shame.[1]

Richard and Elizabeth Edwards had a first son Timothy, whose
life was exemplary; he matriculated at Harvard College in 1691
and earned his degree in 1694; directly after his graduation he
went to a church in East Windsor, Connecticut, a poor village
mission without even an organized congregation, and there he
spent his life doing the Lord's business in a most competent, if
unspectacular, way. In 1732 he had the honor of delivering the
Election Sermon in Hartford and, when the sermon was printed,
of seeing his name on the title-page of his first and only publica-
tion. He was especially well favored in his wife Esther: she was
from a long line of distinguished New England clergy and was
the daughter of the famous Solomon Stoddard, born in 1643 and
for many years minister of the church at Northampton, Massachusetts. She came as a very young bride to East Windsor and
resided long enough in the village to outlive her famous son and
die at the age of ninety-eight. She bore ten daughters and one son,
her fifth child, who received the name Jonathan, perhaps because
it means "gift of Jehovah."

Jonathan Edwards, born in the minister's parsonage on October
5, 1703, spent the first thirteen years of his life under the care of a
strong-willed mother and of a father diligent and patient to make
his son excel in the "things of the Lord." The village of East
Windsor on the banks of the Connecticut River may have been on
the fringe of the wilderness; yet it had many of the middle-class
advantages of a cluster of homes nearer the center of colonial life.
Life there was a life of isolation and hard work; it was also a life
which moved readily with men and women dedicated to make the
will of God and the employments of man's reason work in this
world. The street in which the parsonage stood was fronted by
the homes of citizens who were mindful of their callings to advance the Kingdom of God; and as the village grew in numbers,
its leading citizens prospered, and more books were bought and
read. Increasing pastoral duties required of the Reverend Timothy Edwards more and more time away from home. The educa-
tion of young Jonathan was left, accordingly, in the hands of the
most competent Esther Stoddard Edwards, who drilled him in his

Latin and taught him the rudiments of arithmetic and effective composition.

2

The boy Jonathan's life was marked from the first by a curiosity about the things and the facts of this earth which made him a most precocious youth. To be sure, he was both adventuresome and mischievous: the father, writing from faraway New Haven, counseled the mother to be firm and not to let the boy "Loose w^t he hath Learned" or to be too free with his time. The boy had, however, his own employments; and at the age of twelve he composed a short essay entitled "Of Insects" as witness to his precocity; indeed, it is a most remarkable piece from one so young, and in it was contained the method of thought Jonathan Edwards would follow for a lifetime.[2]

Jonathan had watched spiders at work spinning their webs. He saw that a spider begins by emitting from its body a drop of fluid which congeals in the air and forms a tough and sinuous thread. The fact of spiders' spinning their webs was not of major consequence in the boy's mind; any text in natural history could supply the information on the life of spiders. What concerned Edwards was not only the apparent fact that a spider knows how to make threads and weave them into a web which he uses to catch and hold his food but the answers to two questions which had come to his mind. The first question was: What place do spiders have in the whole insect world they inhabit? He reasoned with himself and soon found an answer.

If all the insects hatched their young in the infinite plenitude with which they lay their eggs, the whole visible world would in time become choked with insects; no other form of life could possibly exist. There must be, however, some law or principle of nature which maintains the insect population in proper balance with the rest of creation. Edwards watched butterflies on the wing and spiders buoyed aloft on their filmy threads and saw that the prevailing westerly winds carried hordes of these insects out to sea where, presumably, they were drowned. To be sure, he avoided the ruthless implication of such a phenomenon; he reasoned, rather, that the movements of these insects are caused not only by air-currents and seasonal changes but by an "intention": spiders are lifted high into the air on filmy threads and traverse extended distances and butterflies have flown across lakes on a principle which can be observed when water floats a piece of wood and trees maintain their upright posture against the wind. Every living object has a tendency, even an intention, to be doing something very like what all other living things are doing. Even inanimate things have "being," for everything is linked along those radial lines which extend from the smallest atom to the infinity of God Himself. The laws of nature merely describe the eternal intention God had for His universe from the beginning of time.

The other question was concerned, not with insects or their behavior in the world, but with human vision. How do we "see" the spiders' webs? Sometimes they are almost invisible; sometimes each thread appears as big as a "cable." Why should this striking difference occur? Is our seeing owing to changes in the physical structure of the spider's web? Surely on the moment of our looking the strand does not suddenly enlarge to the size of a cable; and just as surely the filament does not will that it become visible and invisible, one moment shimmering and iridescent and the next seen hardly at all. Edwards's answer to this curiosity was the correct one: the light from the sun focuses with varying intensity on a solid or translucent object and irradiates from that object with even greater intensity than had the ray which originally lit it. By analogy, a candle set at a distance seems larger than it really is because the light from the flame radiates and disseminates into atmosphere, strikes the particles in the surrounding air (which are otherwise invisible to the naked eye), and thereby appears to cast a much larger glow than the candle flame actually does.

This tentative answer was, however, a dangerous one. If irradiation were a law of nature manifested throughout the universe, then man's vision would be forever the prey of shifting circumstance. Light would not therefore be a constant, an energy, a force; it would be the effects of a stimulus manifested in inscrutably diverse ways on an infinite number of obtruding particles. Every atom, every stone, every piece of glass, every drop of water would give off a differing response to light every moment in time. For one so young, Edwards pursued this problem with tenacity. He reasoned that the dispersal of light from the sun is not simply "light in space"; light is known as light only after it strikes the human retina. The sun shines twenty-four hours of the day, but its light comes to man only in the daylight portion of that time. Furthermore, the near and distant objects are seen in their spatial relationships because the light strikes a near object with greater intensity than a farther object and thus gives it the appearance of nearness and largeness: any man knows that a dust particle before one's eye is not as large as the mountain peak in the distance. How then are these spatial relationships known, and, what is more important, how are they known accurately? Edwards employed one of the best arguments from the new science.[3]

Whether emitted from a source as particles or propagated as waves along a course parallel to the source of its emission, light plays a peculiar part in the activity of nature. Objects are observed to have color; color is not in the objects, else color would disappear once the object was removed. Color is certainly not in the eye of the beholder, else every object would have a differing color, and men would endlessly dispute among themselves concerning the character of red, white, or green. Yet there is observed to be a certain relationship between the particles of natural objects and the particles or waves of light which strike them: the texture of cloth, the sleekness of a film of water, and the outlines of a snowflake are examples of the curious differences between light and substances. Since no object has the "power" (the term is one Edwards would later use) to extract from the surrounding light the luxury of color it desires, then color cannot be generated or even conditioned by the object itself; and since the sum total of all possible colors emitted by the sun is showered upon every natural object, then the function of the object is selective, not creative; the action of any object is limited to sifting and appropriating from that total coloration just those tints which properly belong to it and rejecting all those which do not. An object interferes with and breaks up the colors which strike it, absorbs into itself the color which is rightly its own, and rejects all other colors. That portion of light which objects repel is, according to this theory, what gives them their colors; it is what men see, for they "see" the colors and shadings which the object has repelled.

Human vision is, therefore, generative: it restores to the object those colors which the object had absorbed. It sees the blue or the green because blue and green, even though they have been withdrawn from the bands of light, are still there to be seen by the addition of color which the eye and the mind have known from millions of other objects. Sight organizes; it is ever engaged in assembling units and particles in league with the infinite designs of the universe. Even to see and to know a single unit of substance with its colors requires that one already know the totality to which that part belongs. The discriminating vision sees what is there to be seen and, similarly, is empowered to restore to objects in nature those colors and perspectives which sight does not reveal.

The human mind, like human sight, is a sensitive responder to the world which lies all round it; whatever the activity of nature is, the mind becomes, from its awareness of sense data to the ideas and laws by which life is conducted. But the mind is also self-contained; it is a sensitive organism which is itself continually engaged in sifting through and putting together those impressions which it receives. It is also capable of remaining within its own domain and precincts of thought; it can think about the color blue or about the spider or the butterfly without actually seeing the color or the insect. It can deduce and even prove true laws of behavior and motion without, for days on end, seeing a color or an insect. This power of the mind's thinking within and about itself Edwards early affirmed as the fundamental law of being: while the mind is subservient to the vagaries of force and direction all around it, it is nonetheless ever emboldened to project itself inward, outward, or downward into the infinite sea of speculation and to the farthest verge of eternity. Edwards had reasoned on and proved to himself this principle by means of a theory of optics: his reliance on sight, on vision, was to be a way of speculation for a lifetime. It granted him a personal sensitivity to the vividness of immediate experience; and it provided him with a habit of "seeing" even the most abstruse theological ideas as if they were as clearly apprehended as the sun on its horizon or the leaf turning in the breeze.

Another early schoolboy composition bespeaking the precocity of young Edwards has been conveniently titled "Of Being" by its editors.[4] In it Edwards explored the old argument of beginnings. He phrased the argument in two different ways. One was that of the conjecture concerning absolute Nothing: suppose we could abolish all space, all resistance and solidity, all differentiation between objects, and conceive of an infinite nothing. Yet space would remain "notwithstanding"; there would be the spatial conception necessary even to conceive of the term "Nothing" and "absolute Nothing," for to have a thought one must have "Space" of thinking wherewith to think, even about ultimate nillity. This space and this ultimate, yet indefinable, requisite of thought Edwards defined as God, who becomes that infinite mode and essence of idea even when all other ideas and possible thinking have been resolutely denied or removed. In this way, briefly stated, Edwards proved both the existence of matter as real — for "absolute Nothing" is inconceivable — and the actuality and being of God who becomes, not the mere maker and organizer of His universe, but that ultimate finality of the universe when all else ceases to exist. God therefore exists both as a separate existence and also as the only being who endows objects with their existence.

The other argument in "Of Being" is the reverse of absolute Nothing. It is the principle of an absolute All. Suppose the universe were complete and fulfilled in every detail from the instant of its creation or being. Let "us suppose to illustrate it," Edwards wrote, "that the world had a being from all Eternity, and had many Great Changes and Wonderfull Revolutions, and all the while nothing . . . [and] there was no knowledge in the Universe of any such thing." So to suppose is the most arrant folly: for anything to be known there must be someone to know it. The slightest motion in the world had to be apprehended; the tree which fell in the forest and no one heard was yet known in its falling by the evidence of broken twigs and scattered leaves; and "a Room Close Shut Up that no body sees nor hears nothing in it" is nonetheless known as a closed room by means of all the "effects" it has left. Yet, if no one is actually present to see the tree fall or to perceive the closed room, then how can these things be said to be truly known?

The answer, one of the oldest in logic, is that human consciousness — Edwards used the term as denoting the human mind in all its complex physical, intellectual, and spiritual contexts — suffers from gaps in its thinking. It cannot think all the time; it sleeps, it dreams, it has blanks. Nonetheless, thought is continuous: from hour to hour and day to day the business of thinking proceeds even as the subject of cognition is temporarily abandoned. Then what fills these skipped intermediaries in thought? The answer is, of course, that nature maintains the continuity of thinking even when no one is present. Men are ignorant through long stretches of time; nature proceeds through her "Revolutions" for centuries, and man is ignorant or heedless, even when he is present. But nature, or rather the God who animates all nature, holds thought in reserve until man's mind is ready or nature's activity is propitious in order that just that thought will be released to man in just the way and at just the time he receives it. The Greeks did not discover the circulation of the blood and the Old Testament Jews were not aware of the Copernican theory, not because they were stupid, but because God had not readied the world and the perspective of thought for them. History stands waiting for man, if his thought is of equal worth.[5] Edwards's conclusion is clear: everything that is known, from brute matter to the most sensible of things, is known because it is of itself sensible, it has a "Consciousness" wherewith it can be known. It did not create its being and its mode of being known; it had these qualities bestowed upon it — the stone, the leaf, the door. The giver of all sentience and consciousness is He who alone has being and consciousness, for His being is antecedent to all existence and His thought precedes and directs all thinking. Thus the universe is an ultimate Idea assuming continual form; that which is known is apprehended as a form having shape, space, motion, and definable being; but forms are not fixed and eternal; rather they forever undergo modification, and thus men's ideas, even as new ideas are released in the anticipatory cognition of God, undergo change too. All things are finally emblems, symbols of the primal being which is God. Substance is properly spirit and spirits "Are Properly Substance" in infinite unity of God's universe.

3

In October, 1716, Edwards was one of ten boys who matriculated in the new freshman class at Yale College. This thirteen-year-old son of a Connecticut minister was not destined to live his four years in the cloistered peace of New Haven. Shortly after his arrival, for reasons which have never been fully known, the young men of the freshman class left New Haven and went to Wethersfield, there to place themselves under a certain Elisha Williams. Edwards was one of this migration; and while he showed no signs of rebellion, he seems to have delighted in the instruction he received from the quite brilliant Williams. In October, 1718, by order of the Connecticut assembly, the Wethersfield group of scholar-dissidents returned to New Haven and occupied a new building. Their residence was short, for within a month most of them, but not Edwards, were back in Wethersfield. Owing to the illness of tutor Williams and to further acts of the assembly, the dissidence in the college was settled, and the students were, by 1719, all in residence in New Haven.

Edwards's collegiate studies were doubtless those disciplines which every undergraduate had to endure or master. He studied arithmetic, algebra, Latin, Greek, and Hebrew, rhetoric and logic; he exercised his mind in recitations and taxed his memory with Ames's *Medulla* and *Theological Theses and Cases*, which helped him write sermons later in life. It would be well to know when and how Edwards might have read Berkeley's *Essay Toward a New Theory of Vision*, which was published in 1709, and precisely on what day he first opened Locke's famous *Essay Concerning Human Understanding*; all evidence points to his knowing these works by the time of his second year in college.[6] The mind which read them was youthful, and so was the style in which young Edwards wrote his compositions and made entries in a commonplace book which became known afterward as "The Mind."

The title, "The Mind," which was Edwards's, not that of a subsequent editor, indicates the confident character of the essay.[7] By the time he wrote it, Edwards was in his second year at Yale and had read Locke's *Essay*, a work in which he had as much pleasure as "The most greedy miser" experiences in his newly discovered gold.[8] Edwards found that his early idealism was brought sharply against that mysterious midway region which lies somewhere between the thing as sensed and the mind knowing an idea. Where, then, do ideas "reside"? They cannot, of a certainty, be invented wholly within the mind, nor can they somehow come to have an existence only in the mind without some living relevance to the outside world. The mind cannot invent its awareness of things; something cannot be made from nothing; furthermore, objects in nature do not themselves have sentience or any awareness of themselves. The stone does not know that it is a stone and that it makes on human beings a feeling of hardness, smoothness, or roughness. Objects in nature are known in human minds, not because one stone or one leaf is different from another stone or leaf, but because things are known by means of their relationships to numbers of other objects. The stone is hard, rough, or smooth as its smoothness, roughness, or hardness is part of the sensing of myriads of other specific things—glass, bark on trees, feathers, anything.

Like any other sensitive citizen of his age, Edwards was caught squarely between opposing and contradictory theories concerning the relationship of matter to mind.

On the one hand, the material universe was regarded as eternal, unchanging, and knowable; the observed order must be the only design because God, who could not create order out of nothing, had conceived and fashioned only that one order. Human knowledge was therefore bound to and limited by the eternal Types, the enduring forms, of the divine plan; otherwise, if human thinking could depart from or ever so slightly modify the order, the whole universe would end in mystery. In this view, the human mind is merely another object in unchanging nature; it feels and knows only as it senses the activity of atoms in motion; and the mind, if it is able to think at all, is itself a bundle of atoms in motion and therefore a substance which somehow, even all unaware of what it is doing, "thinks." This might be called the Baconian-Cartesian view; in some respects, when stripped of some of its frank materialism, it was the view of most New England Puritans.

On the other hand, the cosmos came into being and will continue to exist according to some still unrevealed principle beyond man's present knowing. The universe does not appear to be complete; rather, the world of reality seems to contain so many elements and so many jarring variables that to assume the order as man sees it as the supreme handiwork of an all-knowing deity is to do violence both to divinity and to human thought. The mind is, to be sure, a physical substance; but it is not merely a substance and therefore subject to atoms in motion. The human mind is a part of the slowly evolving, eternal motion of all substances proceeding along their routes from chaos to cognition. The mind shares in a divine plan, for it is itself an element in that plan; thus an "idea" is like an atom: each is in some state of coming-to-be — of traveling toward that final consummation of which God is alone aware. Thought and thinking are not, accordingly, forms of natural force; they are occasions wherein the divine activity implicit in all forms of matter comes into some agreement with a man's mind. This might be called the post-Newtonian view. It was this way of a volitional, a "willed" character of life which became for Edwards the major direction of a lifetime.

Because Locke's *Essay* was crucial in the development of Edwards's mind, we might consider the historical climate of opinion in which Locke's thought emerged and then follow the lines which led to Edwards.

4

The *Essay Concerning Human Understanding*, both in its early, synoptic version[9] and in its final edition (1690), shows that

Locke may well have been the first philosopher, if not the first European citizen of international acclaim in the seventeenth century, whose thought had been deeply affected by the travel narratives, the legends of the Indian aborigines, and even the unblushing fabrications which came from America. The recently opened lands far to the west offered Locke the first evidence he or any man had so far found by which the prehistoric past and the outlines of man's thought might be drawn. His aim was, accordingly, to answer on the plenitude of new evidence the important question: Why does the human mind conform to the shape of its geographical location? Is the mind condemned to think only within its racial and natural boundaries, or is it free to move along the lines of its own special cognition? The explorations of the New World suggested that the Indians "contented themselves with the opinions, fashions, and things of their country as they found them, without looking any further." Locke drew a careful difference between "the Virginia king Apochancana" and an educated Englishman: "the difference" was that the Indian's "exercise of his faculties was bounded within the ways, modes, and motions of his own country, and never directed to any other or further inquiries" whereas the Englishman was, even before birth, free of that naturalistic limitation. Locke concluded with a surmise which struck at the center of the question: "And if [the Indian] had not any idea of a God, it was only because he pursued not those thoughts that would have led him to it." [10]

Thinking is not, therefore, the exercise of a divinely bestowed principle of cognition, nor is it a self-willed route of apprehension from one idea to another. Man thinks because he must survive. Just as birds have acquired protective coloration, animals have grown tusks and claws, and vines grow upward along tree trunks, so it was the necessity of man to think. The first occasion of the original thought can never be recovered; yet thinking is traceable to the natural location and to the requirements of the person who thinks; and what men in a time and place think, they will tend to think in that way for a long time to come. "The great difference that is to be found in the notions of mankind," Locke concluded, "is, from the different use they put their faculties to." [11] He was one of the first modern thinkers to realize that history is not the continuing narrative of man's life on this planet but that history is both a mode of thought and a means of apprehending nature. Men are made according to the place in which they live; the very scene and landscape are logistics of thought. History is, therefore, a "disposition": it shapes the human mind and governs the acts of men as they carry on their daily lives, for, to put the theory another way, history is the conjunction of nature and human activity. Thus history is not merely human, nor is it merely naturalistic.

If man thinks because he must survive, then he is but an object in the physical universe and subject to the influences which his world exerts on him; his history and his mind are but the narrative of the rock and the tree and his god a mechanic of an unchanging universe. If, however, man were somehow privileged to direct his mind and to fashion the language he speaks, then some principle of human order might be established by which the natural and the human realms of being could be regarded as both separate and yet united. Indeed, one would depend for its existence and continuity on the other: mind needs nature to have something to think about, and nature profits from the energy of the human mind. Climate and geography and man's responses to his landscape can therefore be considered, not as rigidifying and limiting thought, but as modifying and continuing thought. Human thinking may have its own history, its own rise and fall, even its own life and death quite apart from the natural surroundings in which it occurred.

In a flash of insight Locke anticipated what would become a truism two centuries later: the crudest superstitions are not relics of man's false, and eventually abandoned, thinking; they are stages in the growth of human consciousness; they are the beginnings of man's most profound ideas about himself and his world. The account of man's history might someday show, Locke declared, "how really it may come to pass, that doctrines that have been derived from no better original than the superstition of a nurse, or the authority of an old woman, may, by length of time and consent of neighbours, grow up to the dignity of *principles* in religion or morality." [12] The legend and the taboo might well be the start of the most abstruse, logical thought.

Locke's problem was not, therefore, to prove once again the existence of the human mind. Rather it was to support his assumption that, while the mind obtains its ideas by "sensation" and "reflection," the sensory and the reflective activities proceed in different ways at differing times among different people. Nature conforms to its laws of procedure and continuity; they are, indeed, invariable laws; but human cognition perforce conforms to its own laws and even shows that there are enormous gaps in thinking while men or whole societies are asleep. How then could some principle be found whereby the skipped intermediaries in consciousness could be accounted for? Surely substances are not support for the mind's activity; nevertheless, Locke began his argument with substances.

He sought some way of thinking of objects both as having specific, particular identity and yet as remaining within the natural laws to which all substances conform. A stone or a piece of iron is a discrete object; but the object is known in its stoniness or its iron-like character because of modes and co-ordinates outside itself.[13] The stone does not know its stoniness, nor is the iron aware of its rigidity and density: something other than these observed qualities inheres in the objects and thereby links them to the whole perspective of natural history. In order to account for this apparently dual character of objects, Locke conceived of "primary qualities" and "secondary qualities." When he spoke of "primary qualities," he meant the miscroscopic or physical structure of the object. The "secondary qualities" are, on the other hand, "such qualities which in truth are nothing in the objects themselves but powers to produce various sensations in us by their primary qualities, i.e. by the bulk, figure, texture, and motion of their insensible parts, as colours, sounds, tastes, &c." [14]

"Primary qualities" do inhere in objects; "secondary qualities" are constructs of the human mind in its sensory and reflective response to substances. How, therefore, can the mind conceive of a quality which the object does not have? For if secondary qualities exist only in the mind, they are fictions and therefore untrue. In order to bridge this gap in human cognition, Locke presented the idea of "power." "Power" is the character or tendency of any object to be several things at once: it is a physical substance, a collection of discrete, divisible atoms; it is also that quality of an object to be seen and known with other objects in spatial and temporal relations; and it is, finally, the quality of an object to impart something of itself and thereby to cause a perceiver to sense it. "Power" as sensed is not, however, uniform; any moment of feeling is quite different from another; one instant's speculation on a stone or a piece of iron is just that single incident. Human cognition does not direct "power," for "power" is a force which allows for different, even widely separate, instants of sensing: one does not see the color blue or feel the hardness of stone because he wishes but because he must.

The theory of "power" was an answer to the nagging issue of

the gaps and broken moments in human thought. The "power" which substances manifest in the New World is quite different from the force which objects exert in the Old World. Geography, climate, terrain, even the molecular density of some objects show that forms of matter in America may have gone a special historical route. An archetypal stone or iron is not a correct mode of reasoning about two specimens found in different parts of the world. If there are similarities between objects in the New and the Old Worlds, that likeness is merely a means of reasoning and classification; no genus is irrefutable. This idea was one of Locke's major contributions to cultural thinking: namely, the breakdown of the medieval theory of a total structural analogy existing everywhere simultaneously and uniformly in the universe. In its place Locke offered the principle that matter may be analyzed and made known according to quite differing analogies and contexts.[15] Even the act of thinking, to repeat the truism, is a participant in what is known.

This insight distinguished between the unwilled actions of nature and the "willed" content of the human mind, even as it sought to limit the human will and chart the bounds of human liberty. "Whatsoever modification a substance has, whereby it produces any effect," then "that is called action." Yet "this motion," Locke insisted, "is, when rightly considered, but a passion, if it received it only from some external agent." Since no substance can "begin motion in itself," so, "in thinking, a power to receive ideas or thoughts from the operation of any external substance is called a power of thinking: but this is but a passive power, or capacity." Accordingly, the "power" which causes substances to make impressions on the human mind is not the same "power" which moves the mind to think; thinking concurs in the motions of objects — the mind cannot think apart from its experience with objects; yet thought is not bound within the necessity imposed on it by the insensate substances which are all around it.[16]

Locke's further insight was that the difference between objects and ideas, as well as between the "power" of sensible objects and the "power" which the mind exerts in thinking, was not real or illusory but linguistic. "This reflection," Locke concluded in one of his most telling arguments, "may be of some use to preserve us from mistakes about powers and actions, which grammar, and the common frame of languages, may be apt to lead us into." Language may be the clue to the power of willing man seems to have in a world which nowhere displays a principle of will or choice.

With the evidence he had from hitherto unknown tribes and societies, Locke reasoned that languages are not bestowed as unique endowments on different people. Speech is not savage because it is uttered in a savage tongue or civilized because it is spoken in a civilized language. Men discover and use the words they must have in order to survive in their special portion of the globe; what they afterward record or write depends on how they think. Languages did not begin with simple sounds, for the first grunt of the savage was loaded with profound meaning. Languages began in abstraction; the original sentences were complex combinations. The word "gold," Locke suggested, did not come from a simple awareness of the substance gold; it came from the diverse ways by which mankind has formed its ideas of yellow, ductility, and malleability in association with the substance gold. "This shows how it came to pass," Locke continued, "that there are in every language many particular words which cannot be rendered by any one single word of another. For the several fashions, customs, and manners of one nation . . . which another people have had never an occasion to make, or perhaps so much as take notice of, names come of course to be annexed to them, . . . and so they become so many distinct complex ideas in *their* minds." [17] Language is an artifice determined by use, need, time, and culture. That a European can count to infinity and an American Indian only to twenty does not mean that the American landscape requires a limited arithmetic or that the Indian is naturally stupid; rather, the difference is to be explained by the historic route the two peoples have travelled. Language is, therefore, both a dimension of human culture and a mode of perception: words are expressive of man's daily commonplaces, and they are also ways by which people make the deepest mysteries somehow known to themselves.

Locke's theory of language was the first to show that differences in words between one people and another are not merely differences in human culture but disclosures of the way human intelligence works in particular places. Even though language does not open the universe, it does allow man to look outward upon his world and inward upon himself; in both perspectives he sees that dual vision which he considers real. Locke's theory of a progressive series of forms and symbols functioning in time and place anticipated by several centuries the modern scientific idea of continuity. His principles of the mind and of language also found a ready place in the mind of young Edwards.

5

Human sensing and thinking consist, so Locke had suggested and Edwards realized, of everything that makes up human consciousness — feeling, hearing, tasting, loving, hating, worshipping. They are all the time in concert with the sensing and thinking going on everywhere in the world. Thus everything in the physical and phenomenal universe is linked in one, vast, mysterious universe of "thought." All thought and every idea exist, therefore, in some tentative, provisional, forever unresolved state of similarity and dissimilarity, of immediacy and of abstraction, of partial ignorance and of partial knowing. The rule of thinking Edwards appropriately defined as "the consent of being to being, or of being's consent to entity." Knowledge emerges tentatively — quite on its own and without the effect of any human mind — weaves with other and disparate knowledge, enlarges, foliates, and moves outward as though from its original center. Like light rays, it is deflected, it bends around obstacles; but always it moves, sometimes losing and sometimes gaining force just as light rays are refracted or intensified in the eye of the beholder. "Yea," Edwards reasoned, "there must be an universal attraction in the whole system of things from the beginning of the world to the end. . . . So that these things must necessarily be put in to make complete the systems of the ideal world." [18]

From the early essay "Of Insects" through "The Mind," Edwards showed the double character of his intellectual world in which he lived and the double character of his mind. He exhibited, on one side, an empiricist's awareness of the power and purity of sense impressions; they are, after all, the source and impetus for thought. On the other hand, he demonstrated the idealist's declared intention not to remain merely in things-as-they-are: objects and ideas may necessarily agree, for the object is the start and the continuation of any idea. Yet an idea had somehow to be either in existence or in some form of comprehension even before the object came into being: the stoniness of the stone antedates the stone. God from His side, Edwards reasoned, has designed those motions and incentives which are felt by the body and become ideas in the mind. God, not the stone, was the origin of the physical properties of the stone and the eventual and usable idea of its stoniness. Body and mind are continually acted upon by differing powers and influences; thinking consists, not of units and divisibles of thought conforming to a route of motion and inevitability like the life-history of atoms, but of indeterminate, unresolved clusters and even ambiguities of thought. To live in bodily excitement and vividness is to live in what Edwards called "essential good": body and mind are conjoined in every act, every idea, every moral decision. At a stroke Edwards disavowed any difference between "natural" and "supernatural" knowledge. Knowing is a daily process, not an inexplicable occurrence like magic; knowing begins in the apprehended fact, continues through the mind's apprehension of its ideas and its own being, and ends with man's realization of his place in the eternal God-willed universe.

The argument may be old, the lines of support or denial well known, and yet the young Edwards had in his 'teens begun in the commonplace world of daily, sensed fact — the objective fact of the spider and its web, the dew clinging to the grass blade, the pendant drop of water after rain on a bush or tree, the motion of winds, and the flights of insects in shimmering clouds through the air. Even before he entered Yale College, Edwards was in a time of vividness and exhilaration like that of a youthful poet, even a Keats; yet he was exhilarated not only by the facts of little and wondrous things but by what is more important, the activity of a mind capable of knowing and discovering a world quite on its own. For the senses are merely the windows of the mind; they are given to man fresh and even free each time a human being is born. A man at any age should be able to come alive each morning, to stand on tiptoe against the sun's rising or the rain's falling, and to close each day as if nothing like it had ever existed before or would ever come again; one could thank God for the nearly intoxicating revel of the senses, for God had given them to man and they were nearly divine.

The ideas of John Locke and the reading of *An Essay Concerning Human Understanding* had had the effect of opening the eyes of young Edwards. The senses cannot be anything else but good, for they are the first ways we can know God and His world; and the route of one's cognition, from the sense impression to the idea in the mind, is both good and wondrous beyond compare. Yet this remarkable boy was too wise to remain all his life in the sweet delight of sunrise, rainbow, or glistening spiders' webs. From Locke he had learned one crucial lesson: the world and the way of the senses are "caused." The mind does not create the rainbow or the sunset; one does not decide for himself on some splendid day that stones are hard and feathers are soft. If one so much as cuts his finger, he does so because certain facts and events are placed in just the order to bring the knife-blade in touch with flesh.

Edwards realized that the cause of sensing and of ideas is not, however marvellous the time and however awake the mind, an occasion of just that moment's impact and knowing. "Cause" is a condition of history; it is old as the universe and as endless as the mind of God: even so commonplace an event as the sparkle of a speck of dust is out of infinite causes which extend through time. Thus rightly to define "cause" Edwards had to trace every moment's sensing and every idea in the mind back to the original causation of God. Such an interminable tracing would be, of course, impossible: the mind is confined to this present; no one can penetrate the abyss of history or know the origins of God's thought. But one can know, if he seeks hard and far enough, the cause and the possible route of one's own sensings and ideas. Thus Edwards was, all the while that his mind moved along the way of Locke's design, a proper Puritan: he was impelled continually to seek the origins of his mind in those instantaneous flashes wherein God, from His side, might be revealing Himself to the children of men. Why God should choose just that moment no one could know; but one could be awake and ready for the possibility which God offered in the commonest event of sunrise and bird flight. To live in the senses was, therefore, to live not only in wonder — the newly created wonder of atoms in motion and the mind in its thought — but also to live in design, proportion, symmetry, or what Edwards called "excellency." "Excellency" had special connotations for the young Edwards; it is, he wrote, "not merely equality and proportion, but any kind of similarness"; it is the "beauty" which "consists in similarness or identity of relation"; it is the "correspondence" which begins in little simple things, reaches outward and upward through clusters and aggregates of things just as atoms make up the "consistency" of rocks, and finally extends to and includes the mind and being of God. Yet the being of God is not simply the awesome consciousness of the universe: the being and "excellency" of God are radial lines extending downward and outward from that center of the universe which is both everywhere and nowhere.[19]

Edwards's early appeal is to wakefulness and to wonder. "Knowing" begins in the single fact, continues through the mind's apprehension of its ideas and its being, and ends with man's realization of his special place in the eternal God-willed universe. This call to wakefulness and this appeal to the uniqueness of the mind would be Edwards's theme for a lifetime. His years in college and the early period of his ministry were adventures along this way.

2

Sovereign God and Reasoning Man

DURING his undergraduate years Edwards began to keep a record of his daily life contained under a set of double entries. One he called "Resolutions"; these were advices to himself, statements of his condition on this or that day, and exhortations that he strive to do better than he had been doing. Some of these notations were in the manner of any young man — Benjamin Franklin perhaps — advising himself on ways of becoming successful: "Never to lose one moment of time, but to improve it in the most profitable way I possibly can"; or, "To maintain the strictest temperance, in eating and drinking." [1] The tone is so well-known in the lives of successful men that these entries seem hardly more than codicils in the documents of the American dream. Most of them are, however, of quite a different character, for they were jottings made in keeping with and at the same time as a "Diary" Edwards began in December, 1722, and maintained intermittently for two years. They range over a wide variety of meditation, insight, speculation, wonder, joy, and despair; they form one of the most interesting and valid records we have of Edwards's mind in one of its crucial periods.

Over and over again Edwards stressed the absolute importance of a man's belief in God's sovereignty. It was a doctine he made into a keystone of his own theology, and it was one that, when he became a minister, he drilled into his hearers as the primary necessity for their salvation. Yet much as he later came to "love" that doctrine, the youthful Edwards felt a strong repugnance to it: "From my childhood up," he wrote later in his *Personal Narrative*, "my mind had been full of objections against the doctrine of God's sovereignty, in choosing whom he would to eternal life, and rejecting whom he pleased; leaving them eternally to perish, and be everlastingly tormented in hell. It used to appear like a horrible doctrine to me." [2] Here was the great stumbling block in the way of his personal faith; no amount of reasoning could overcome it. Indeed, reason was but another obstacle in the solving of this great issue. Faith, and faith alone, was the way out of the difficulty; but a man might wait a lifetime to gain enough faith, and his end might find him still resisting and unrepentant.

At the time of his greatest resistance to this doctrine, the youthful Edwards was twice afflicted with illness; once it was a pleurisy sometime before he entered Yale College; the second occasion was in 1725. In both instances Edwards feared, as his Resolutions and Diary suggest, not that he would die: death seems not to have darkened his mind as he lay helpless; rather, he feared that he might not find in the illness and affliction that humility of mind and soul which was the first requisite for overcoming his resistance. Arrogance of heart, willful self-righteousness, the young man's passionate need for self-realization and self-fulfillment — these were the darkenings of the way which Edwards knew he must travel before he could finally recognize the truth that God is Almighty and that man is even less than the blade of grass or the speck of dust. God's sovereignty was a gospel truth; it was also the first test of a man's seeking salvation; and it was, most importantly, the primary condition for self-knowledge. To be abased and to rise, to be humbled until one cried in anguish and then to be lifted up by that very power one had feared and even loathed, was the central act in Christian experience. Whatever one's destiny in life, one did not shape one's course; everything one did, from the first infant's cry to the last gasp of mortal life, was foreordained by a deity who, if He should vary His intention by so much as a single atom's motion, would deny His godhead. Thus God's sovereignty is not only what one is as a human being, but it also measures what one is not in the eyes of God. It echoes Luther's cry when he fell in a faint in the choir loft, "*Ich bin's nit! Ich bin's nit!*" or "*Non sum! Non sum!*", either of which can be translated "It's not I" or "I am not." [3]

The nearly violent opposition to the idea of God's sovereignty was very like Satan's and the unregenerate man's hatred of God. It was the presence of that dross and waste in life, that unbidden fear of losing one's spiritual energy and of "falling away," which haunted Edwards in his youth and demanded of him the most arduous exertions. When he could not meet that exacting requirement, he weakened and became ill. Yet the illness had a palliative and recovering force; for in the descent of the flesh to the submission of sickness, that dark and obsessive resistance to the true light was softened. In the second of the two major illnesses (that of 1725 which laid him low "for about a quarter of a year") "God was pleased," he afterward recalled, "to visit me again, with the sweet influences of his Spirit. My mind was greatly engaged there in divine pleasant contemplations, and longings of soul. I observed that those who watched with me, would often be looking out wishfully for the morning . . . ; and when the light of day came in at the windows, it refreshed my soul from one morning to another. It seemed to me some image of the light of God's glory." The recovery and the acceptance of God's sovereignty came about because of what William James called "letting go"; Edwards did not think; he simply felt, and the presence of God's being became apparent. Thus, after his recovery from the illness, he wrote: "The doctrines of God's absolute sovereignty, and free grace, . . . and man's absolute dependence on the operations of God's Holy Spirit, have very often appeared to me as sweet and glorious doctrines. These doctrines have been much my delight." [4]

The awesome doctrine of God's sovereignty — a subject on which, as we shall see, Edwards wrote his first published work — was counterbalanced for Edwards in these early years by several modes of thought. One was his understanding of mental perception by means of his assumptions of and revisions in Locke's theory of the mind. Another, perhaps equally important, was what Edwards knew from British thinkers who had already considered the question of God's incoming spiritual light. Among these were the group known as the Cambridge Platonists — Ralph Cudworth chiefly, but also Henry More and Benjamin Whichcote. Indeed, Edwards inherited the intellectual foreground of seventeenth-century English Puritans; as one commentator has correctly stated, there is "little distinction . . . between the writers of New England and the particular English theologians and teachers of the . . . seventeenth century under whom New Englanders studied, whom they read and digested before their migration and continued to read for over a century thereafter." Nothing supports this statement better than Edwards's "Catalogue of Books" with its many references to seventeenth-century British religious writers. In this list the name of Richard Baxter, the English theologian, appears seven times, one less than the references to Newton and one more than to Locke's name; the thought of Baxter can be taken as part of the intellectual and spiritual ancestry of Edwards's ideas.[5]

Yet Edwards's reading in the English theologians was not

wholly for the confirmation of ideas he already had; apparently he was attracted to these books because they spoke to him in a language he was himself using. God's sovereignty and His majesty in the world were not merely dogmas: they were modes of feeling; they were activities of the senses. Even though the language of Baxter and others may come from Scripture and from the great tradition of Christian apologetics stemming from Augustine, the words have a haunting resonance and a design which make them felt and seen. The references to light and to color are regular and pervasive. For Baxter "the Spirit giveth light"; for John Owen, "Light requires neither proofe nor Testimony for its Evidence. Let the Sun arise in the firmament, and there is no need of Witnesses to prove and confirm unto a seeing man that it is day." Light does not seize and envelop a man, as it did in Augustine's vision of God's power; rather, light explains the continuing effects which God's world has on the intransigent or the enlightened man; it may shine into the heart and transform a man's life. Thus for Baxter and the Cambridge Platonists light is a link in thought between the act of intuition by which grace is received and the continuing effects on the senses with which a man lives. Human reason arrives at a knowledge of God and, at its best, reaches salvation when it is moved from without and when it comes to open its lifelong dialogue with the world of facts and ideas.

This sensuous and, by turns, mystical activity is nowhere better disclosed in Edwards's youthful writings than in that extraordinary paragraph which has afterward been known as "Sarah Pierrepont."

Edwards wrote it when he was twenty. The girl was only thirteen. To the modern reader, to express love for a presumably gracious and lovely young woman by recounting that girl's extraordinary sensitivity to divine impulses seems strange indeed. The single paragraph of approximately one hundred words tells us almost nothing about the person who was Sarah Pierrepont; it does tell us a great deal about Jonathan Edwards in this crucial time of his life when he was seeking some sense of his place and being in the world.

The curious opening of the confession — "They say there is a young lady in [New Haven] who is beloved of [the] Great Being . . ." — suggests that the writer is himself at a distance and unempowered to approach or write about such a saintly being. The distance is metaphysical only; for the movement of the confession is away from the brusqueness, the sternness, the masculinity of the world and ever toward the sweetness, sensitivity, and delicacy of the woman's appreciation: "this Great Being, in some way or other invisible, comes to her and fills her mind with exceeding sweet delight. . . . She expects after a while," the meditation goes on, "to be raised up . . . out of the world and caught up into heaven. . . . There she is to dwell with him, and to be ravished with his love and delight forever." [6] The tone is that of the rapture of the flesh and the mystical wonder which come to the soul, both well known in the writings of Christian saints; the commonplaces of ecstasy are all through the brief and tantalizing paragraph.

The crux of the confession is its opposition to the formal statements Edwards was writing on the doctrine of God's sovereignty. Sarah Pierrepont is a refuge from the harshness, the terror, and the abject feeling of inconsequence which came to Edwards every time he pondered that awesome question of God's infinite majesty. The "objections" and resistances to the sovereignty of God broke down not only because Edwards made his peace with the domineering image of the father which loomed so long for him but because the wondrous joy and delicacy of the feminine counterpart to God the Father came in the form and the presence of an extraordinary girl who, as Edwards wrote of her, "is of a wonderful sweetness, calmness and universal benevolence of mind; especially after this Great God has manifested himself to her mind. She will sometimes go about from place to place, singing sweetly; and seems to be always full of joy and pleasure. . . ." [7]

The figure of the woman, whether saintly or earthly, has been for ages man's refuge from the brute realities of himself and his world. The Roman Church had long made this feminine gentleness a dogma, for the Mother sat at the right hand of God as an intercessor for fallible men on this earth. Edwards may be discovering what human longing had once resolved in a doctrine; but, as in so many things, Edwards had to discover the meaning for himself. That he discovered it in the person of the young woman with whom he would enjoy the privileges of the nuptial bed might suggest a lurking tendency to masquerade fleshly desires behind the vesture and rhetoric of spirituality, even mystical rapture. Yet as men have long known, flesh and spirit are in mystical experience and in mystical writing so close as to be indistinguishable. The ravishment which Sarah enjoyed with God was not very far from the physical union she would have with her young husband; and the young Edwards's ecstatic vision of his beloved in the passionate fulfillment with God was little different from his own erotic-mystical dream. Men do not deceive themselves and find their frustrated yearnings in sublimated guises of the union of the soul with God; they find resolutions for their deepest despairs in evocations which, for a time, appease their doubts and relieve their fallen hopes. From the sovereign father and God to the winsome, alluring, spiritualized girl, Edwards moved from the darkness into the light. It was, perhaps, not quite the light of this world, but it was light nevertheless and it shone all the more brightly for its being lodged in a person of such appeal and wonder.

The light which shines throughout "Sarah Pierrepont" is not only the light of God's benign grace; it is also a rhetorical brightness, a language of wonder and joy and love which would become, in the after years of Edwards's ministry, one of the key manners of his preaching style. The device is the vision of sinful man ringed with the brilliant light of God's restoring grace; man can do nothing for himself; the light does all. But, on the instant or for the hour of its shining, miracles are wrought, and anguished man knows, however fitfully and briefly, that he is saved of God. Edwards developed a meditative style which begins with "Sarah Pierrepont" and remained with him throughout his life.

One sign of this style is Edwards's poetic eye-mindedness; it is a Romantic poet's insistence that the object is the word, and the word is the instant conveyor of the object to the inward sight of the mind. The paragraph is keyed to a language of seeing: light shines, the darkness flees; the girl goes about, she sees and is full of sweet delight; the paths and the groves are ringed with joy, and the unseen becomes a presence as real as if it were there to be touched. The verbs are all in the present tense, a now of seeing and speculation, as if everything from the past to the future could be lived instantly; the radiance of the girl's presence is like the line between visibility and invisibility and between what "seems" and "is." If the modern reader misses the stages in comprehension, the tension between the slowly opening wonder and the dazzling fulfillment, Sarah Pierrepont was for Edwards the soul's immediate presence in divine things. God fills His universe, and His presence is there to be known. Man, feeble and obtuse, resists the moment, but this divinely inspirited girl sees everything.

"Sarah Pierrepont" is indeed very close to Edwards's meditations on spiders and his conjectures on "The Mind." They have the same subject: the mind's and the soul's apprehension of divine things. In "Sarah Pierrepont" Edwards had, as it were, someone else to undergo the experience for him and then stand on the other side waiting for him to follow. In his more formal and logical excursions on this question Edwards had to present the experience as he was living it. Yet in both instances the emphasis is on the mind's seeing — on a visionary present of such intensity that things are not merely felt and known; they are seen as mediatorial relevances between what lies like dross in the mind and what exists forever in the phenomenal universe of God. The meditation is swift, hardly more than an instant, but in its coming it suddenly invests the world with splendor and light, and in its going it leaves the mind just that much more alive than it was. The visionary dream of "Sarah Pierrepont" was Edwards's poem to the most elevated and intoxicating physical response to the world; that he should have put his dream of wonder in the person of a young girl might suggest his unwilling awareness bordering on shame that he was seldom, if ever, in his own life and being, capable of such ecstasy.

The doctrine of God's sovereignty was the counterstatement to wonder; it was that dark, unbidden side of a young man's life when the despair became a real illness and the doubt was like the coming of the night. Indeed, the doctrine of God's sovereignty might well represent the mind against the flesh; it could also spell, as Edwards's later life disclosed, a waning of his power of visionary insight: the world became less and less ringed with light, and the remarkable young man's responses to the physical world faded. Despite several occasions when he may have felt the coming and then the presence of the Light, Edwards never again had quite the visionary ecstasy of "Sarah Pierrepont." The girl became the woman; the young man became an older man; and, with the waning of a profound awareness of this world in all its magic and divine grace, Edwards slowly lost what he had so much enjoyed in his youth. The dogmatist and, more especially, the intellectual disputant triumphed over the poet, not because an angry God shut the valves of the youth's attention but because Edwards suffered that inevitable wastage of sensual delight. As it left him, he did what many another first-class mind has done: he tended, as we shall see, more and more to intellectualize perception and to fashion, not vivid lineaments of this world in its light, but well-lighted principles and fully seen ideas.

Edwards was learning, both by living it and writing about it, the meditative way. It is a "way," and each man must learn it for himself. In Edwards's time it had been so long practiced in England and America that a sensitive young person hardly needed to look beyond the shelves of books in his home or in his school library to find texts for comparison and instruction. Indeed, the manner of meditation had become a mode of poetry which the English poets of the sixteenth and seventeenth centuries had exhibited with such imagination that a poet like the Puritan Edward Taylor had found it wholly effective to his thought. Each Sunday he penned his Preparatory Meditation in verse on the same text he had used in his sermon: a formal, logical disquisition from the pulpit was one way of presenting an idea; but a quiet, inner colloquy with oneself was another, and perhaps the second was more necessary to the soul's vitality than the first.

What Edwards learned in his young manhood was not only the meditative manner — the apposite phrasing of a thought, however that thought might bear overtones of Scripture, and the location of that thought in the recesses of one's private being — but a meditative style. The style is not easily apparent in Edwards's Diary and Resolutions, for they are couched in a language which bears all the colors of copybooks and good advice. Yet the beginnings and the development of that style are there nonetheless.

Edwards learned that experience, which necessarily comes from the outside (Locke had proved that truth), turns inward: it moves from fact to idea, from substance to concept; it conforms to a logic which God has implanted in His universe since the beginning of time. Yet the inward turning of experience is the translation of facts and human acts into words. The use of the right word, the turn of the phrase, the winding of the thought through a sentence could be the tentative or ultimate resolution of that activity God has implanted in His universe and the intelligence He expects men to develop. A word, a sentence, a paragraph or a page could be that ever-widening possibility for the mind to live within itself or to go outward and do the work which it should perform. Edwards thus began in his youth to develop a style which would open the world and yet which would somehow relate that world to one's own will. To the extent that words can organize, however variously and even for a time falsely, a realm of meaning, then words are man's way to control fate.

Thus Edwards's style had a limpidity and grace, even from the beginning, which are missing from other Puritan meditative writings. The Lockean effect was already apparent: words are not simply "real" reflections of real things; they are relevances which the mind establishes between itself and what lies all around it. As relevances they may relate only as God has prescribed — for God, in the beginning, made the Word just as He made atoms; nevertheless, the possibility for variety and for fresh incentives is endless. Words became, therefore, modes of discovery — a discovery of objects in relation to the world and of ideas which only those words, in just their right order, could convey. In 1725 Edwards noted: "There are a great many exercises, that for the present, seem not to help, but rather impede, Religious meditation and affections, the fruit of which is reaped afterwards, and is of far greater worth than what is lost; for thereby the mind is only for the present diverted; but what is attained is, upon occasion, of use for the whole life-time." It was not the impediment or the diversion which mattered; it was the "affection" or the soul's learning which could be "reaped afterwards" that made the difference, and the only means of so catching thought in its passage was to give it its true and memorable word. Even Edwards's private, cautionary advices to himself are couched in this ambience of meditative possibility: "A virtue which I need in a higher degree," he noted, "to give a beauty and lustre to my behaviour, is gentleness. If I had more of an air of gentleness, I should be much mended." [8] Edwards's style was a way of turning experience in upon one's self and of refining that sensible comprehension into the language of introspection. Words became the ever-widening and ever more personal possibility that one could, and indeed must, build a world from within.

2

Edwards took his B.A. degree at Yale in 1720 and resided at the college two years afterward in order to prepare himself for the ministry. In 1722, as the result of an application of some ministers in New York, he was licensed to preach, and in August went to New York, where he remained for eight months. He lived happily in the house of a Mrs. Smith and became a good friend of her son, John Smith. In 1724 Edwards accepted a Yale tutorship, beginning his duties in June of that year. The subsequent two-year period in his life, however briefly Edwards described it, was marked by great distress of spirit. For one thing,

Edwards missed his good friend John Smith in New York. More importantly, he was in some mood which gave him "abundant reason to be convinced of the troublesomeness and vexation of the world, and that it will never be another kind of world." [9] He charged himself with listlessness of body and mind; he was afflicted with strange attacks of an illness which, after a healthy youth, seemed strange indeed but which was to be with him for the remainder of his life. Undoubtedly the main cause of his weariness and distress was a sense of falling away from the high and moving spiritual incentive he had felt three and four years earlier; in the *Personal Narrative*, written some twenty years afterward, Edwards remembered this dark time in his life when his spirit was dull and had not the insight it once seemed to have. In 1726 he confessed that " 'Tis just about three years, that I have been for the most part in a low, sunk estate and condition, miserably senseless to what I used to be, about spiritual things." [10] He became at that time so ill that he retired to East Windsor throughout the spring and early summer of that year, returning to the Yale tutorship in the autumn.

Fortunately, a change and relief were near: when the congregation of Northampton, Massachusetts, was casting about for a successor to the aging and distinguished Solomon Stoddard, an invitation came to Edwards to be a candidate for the position. Five months later, on February 15, 1727, he signed his name to the Northampton Town Book in token of his acceptance of the call; and on July 20 he and Sarah Pierrepont were married in the Northampton church. [11] That the well-loved Solomon Stoddard was in his eighty-fourth year, had served his people for fifty-five years, and was Edwards's grandfather only increased the necessity that the young assistant prove himself. Nevertheless, the early years of Edwards's ministry were happy ones: even if he was not yet twenty-four years old when it began, and certainly came under the onus of speaking in a voice which ill accorded with the noble tones of his grandfather, Edwards did speak with such fervor and authority that even those skeptical of new ideas were impelled to listen. Then, in February, 1729, Stoddard died and was laid to rest.

In his day Stoddard had brought great dismay to the clergy, particularly those in and around Boston, by his frank declaration that no tests on earth could possibly reveal the state of a man's soul and that to make a man stand before the church, "profess" his faith, and then solemnly undergo an inquiry by the church smacked of the most impious tyranny and moral obtuseness. Only God could look into the soul; and only the man himself, moved by the profoundest workings of God's spirit and witnessing to the transformation that had occurred in his life, could testify to his redemption. Thus Stoddard had allowed people to join the holy community who had not passed through the witness to their salvation; during a number of extraordinary revivals he had conducted or which had apparently risen spontaneously in the Connecticut Valley, Stoddard had brought many into the church without the accredited tests of their conviction and holiness. Indeed, he had gone even farther: he had declared that no man could deny another the privilege of partaking of the holy elements of the Communion; should a man of sinful life and impure soul eat of the bread and the wine, then he condemned himself, all the while that the community of saints was untouched. In his preaching and in his ministry to his people, Stoddard had emboldened and empowered men in ways which made Northampton and the neighboring portion of the Connecticut Valley one of the admired places for the surprising works of God.

The first occasion for the young Edwards to appear on a larger scene than that of Northampton came when he was invited to preach in Boston at "the Publick Lecture" a sermon which he delivered on July 8, 1731. It was entitled *God Glorified in the Work of Redemption, by the Greatness of Man's Dependence upon Him, in the Whole of It.* It earned such favor that some of the clergy requested that it be printed; it was Edwards's first published work.

3

God Glorified is, quite simply, a study in human thought at the very beginning of self-understanding. It is *self*-understanding; it is not an awareness of God, for He is as remote at the end of Edwards's argument as at the outset. The beginning of man's slavation is in Christ's saying, "Except a man be born again, he cannot see the Kingdom of God." Edwards did not so much as allude to this central mystery in Christian living; rather he used as a text the words of Paul, "He that glorieth, let him glory in the Lord." A paraphrase might be, He that would become and would know, he must realize himself in his debasement and triviality. It is the life of man looked at from the smallest end of visionary distance and God viewed from the ultimate remove. Edwards sets up what would often be a curious polarity in his thinking: if he could see the most awesome being of God in the farthest extent of space, then he might be able to see the instant present, the infinitesimal self of man. Even if the distance is unbridgeable — what coordination can be found between the finite and the infinite? — somewhere in the vastness of time and speculation lies a link, a clue to be held and known in the mind. Thus from this visionary distance God confers on dependent man the possibility of living and knowing beyond mere human existence.

But how? Edwards sought an answer in a problem left from Locke's epistemology: what is the ground and source of our knowledge and our being? The answer was, of course, quite simple; it was God. But to say that God is the origin of all our being and of our knowledge of the world is merely to repeat a platitude which any school child can echo. What aspect of God was this origin? It could not be the whole of God, for He never reveals to men His blinding light; it was not the manifestation of God in the daily working of nature, else worship and knowledge of Him would be an easy pantheism or, in terms contemporary with Edwards's age, deism: God manifests Himself in His works; therefore He is best loved and served by working in His world. Edwards would spend a lifetime countering this nimble and delusive syllogism; he could deal with it summarily here.

The aspect of God which God has willed for man to appreciate and come to know is His sovereignty. The word denoted not only God's awesome and eternal power but also His scrupulous regard for just that portion of His all-encompassing majesty which man is capable of knowing. Just as Locke had sought to delimit the vaulting ambition of human intellect, Edwards essayed to reduce man to just that triviality, that residue of being which is left over after all that is not-God or anti-God is stripped away. That which is anti-God is human; it is the taint which mankind forever inherits as the sin of the first parent; it is also the darkness of soul, the egregious surge of the mind when it thinks it can know anything, even itself, on its own.

Quite in accord with Locke's theory of the mind, Edwards proposed that man is dependent "on God's goodness" for everything that he has, just as the sensible world provides every stimulus for an impression on the senses and every image lodged in the mind. God's sovereignty is therefore the physical law of the universe: whether man does good works or bad works no more casts doubt on God's sovereignty than good works and ill reflect on or deny the presence of impressions made on the eye, the ear, the nose, or the fingertips. The principle of sovereignty is that first law before all other laws; on it we depend for our life and our natural being.

But if God's sovereignty were the only law of the universe and the only manifestation of His divine being, then we would never have been raised above the level of the beasts, who surely acknowledge a power higher than themselves; they are subject to the invariable rules of birth, vitality, and death. Man was given a special privilege and designation: at some time in his history (and it may well have been a "time") man became aware of himself; he had the power of seeing himself in some association with the world around him; he came to have a sense of his low or high estate, of his shame, of his pride, and, most importantly, of his littleness in the awful majesty of the creation he was permitted to inhabit. It was, quite simply, the pleasure principle which gave man his first inkling of his littleness. "So the production of the effect," Edwards said, "is sensible." We fear first, we love afterward; we fall down, we then rise; we quake with terror at the eclipse and the lightning, we then comprehend. "We are more apparently dependent on God for happiness, being first miserable, and afterwards happy. It is more apparently free and without merit in us, because we are actually without any kind of excellency to merit. . . . All our good is more apparently from God, because we are first naked and wholly without any good, and afterwards enriched with all good." [12] The first provision of God's sovereignty is the Covenant of Works or of the sensible world as it is.

Man's next and higher stage of cognition is the sensible, "inherent" workings of God's sovereignty in the human soul. This is not a level or stage in consciousness; what is an "objective good" known to the senses is in no wise different, potentially, from the "inherent good" known in the soul. Body, mind, and soul accord in the total activity which is consciousness; even if the world seems to be apart from the cognitive action of the mind, it only "seems": to suppose a division in the mental and intellectual faculties of man is to presume a split in the phenomenal universe of God. Thus "inherent good" is in all objects; and so too does "objective good" exist in the most airy speculations of the mind and soul. For what the mind and the soul know they know objectively: the Word, any word, is an objective perception — man sees, feels, tastes, hears, and touches it, else he does not know it at all. God's power is a "sensible" power; holiness is a perceptible state; man lives his days in vivid contact with a universe which everywhere has meaning. The renewed sense of life and of being is, once it comes to the deserving man, "a more glorious work of power than mere creation, or raising a dead body to life, in that the effect attained is greater and more excellent. That holy and happy being," Edwards continued, "is a far greater and more glorious effect, than mere being and life. And the state from whence the change is made . . . is far more remote from the state attained, than mere death or nonentity." [13]

Edwards's aim in the second half of the sermon is to make a theory of perception — his objective idealism, that is — accord with the new logic of continuity. It was a "new logic" in that it derived from Bacon's inductive method and presupposed that for every logical continuity in thought there is of necessity a prior logic in nature and in idea. Man cannnot think from A to B or, farther, to X unless he has already been provided with a systematic prescription for following that line of reasoning. Man cannot suppose hypotheses about absolutes and entities if he cannot locate any actual entities and definable absolutes in the world. And, just as certainly, thought cannot proceed from cause, to effect, to end, unless the method can be known in atoms and molecules which themselves demonstrate the action of cause, effect, and end.[14]

Edwards supposes a causative principle which works, if not invariably, to an end. That principle is the dependence of men on God: "They have all their good of him, and . . . they have all through him, and . . . they have all in him: That he be the cause and original whence all goodness comes, therein it is *of* him; and . . . he be the medium by which it is obtained and conveyed, therein they have it *through* him; and . . . he be that good itself that is given and conveyed, therein it is *in* him. Now those that are redeemed by Jesus Christ do, in all these respects, very directly and entirely depend on God for their all." [15] The argument is derived from and proceeds along a visionary continuity from *of* to *through* to *in;* its direction is the dramatic implication of man and his soul in the antecedent being of God on Whom man depends for everything that he is. The logic is visualized as an infinite perspective with God at the farthest remove in space and time, yet He is in full, encompassing control of and participation in His world in which man is an infinitesimally small unit whose very life and being depend both on the distance which God maintains and the instant apprehension He allows. It is a picture very like some of the extraordinary ceiling and dome paintings of the Renaissance, wherein as one looks upward he sees the whole visible distance open and assume form and color; while the painting may stop at the walls which support the heavenly view, the scene nevertheless gives the distinct illusion that not just the ceiling or the upward space but the whole visionary distance as far as the eye can see in any direction has been opened. The space of control is thus infinite and particular: the upward heaven is aglow with light, but the single figure looms with portentous importance.

Thus along this infinite visionary perspective Edwards could see and array the need for and the occasion in personal salvation. The stress was on personal salvation: God from His distance and at His mere pleasure chose to select and save man. He did so, not because He was present at all instants in the terrestrial world of man, but because He, from aloft and on high, suspended and sustained the visual world below. He could at His will move into it and absent Himself from it. Edwards is not concerned with prudential morality: that will come as a subsidiary of indwelling grace. What he is trying to prove is that God's sovereignty and omnipotence are universal, grand, and awesome and that man's deserving is unwilled, trivial, and beggarly. It is only because man is infinitely small and unworthy, because he is lodged far from God in the visionary perspective, and because he cannot do anything of himself to bring about his possession of grace that God wills the salvation of His child. "The grace of God in bestowing this gift is most free. It was what God was under no obligation to bestow." And again: "It is more apparently free and without merit in us, because we are actually without any kind of excellency to merit, if there be any such thing as merit in creature excellency. And we are not only without any true excellency, but are full of, and wholly defiled with, that which is infinitely odious." [16]

Man could rise from nothing to something because he is truly nothing; but he must first acknowledge his nothingness; human life is insufficient because God is all-sufficient and provides it with its only sufficiency: "We have the greater occasion to take notice of God's all-sufficiency, when all our sufficiency is thus every way of him. . . . Such a dependence on God demonstrates God's all-sufficiency." Man exalts himself, he debases God and thereby denigrates the God that is in him; as he debases himself the more surely he will "be disposed to exalt God." The "disposition" of man to look favorably upon himself is thus the great foe of self-knowledge: man must fall in order to rise; he must be ignorant — truly and knowingly ignorant — in order that he may know.[17]

The cogency of this argument, as Edwards had himself reasoned in his Resolutions and Diary, was that the probability and the activity of man's salvation were turned inward upon man himself. God's redeeming grace did not come as an absolute gift from the outside; it was not lodged in formal doctrine nor even in the Holy Word; it was placed wholly in the individual consciousness of any man who truly lives and truly seeks to know. Salvation began, therefore, as self-understanding; except a man know himself he cannot know God. Yet knowing one's self was perilous in the extreme: self-knowledge might bring immoderate desire, ambition, pride, or even the bland *acedia* of the spirit when man convinces himself of his all-sufficiency. Thus Edwards could not chart the lines of man's understanding of himself and of God: the adventure is different every time it occurs. No man can be a guide to another, no word is enough to distill the truth. Only by seeing himself as fallen, as far in the darkness of God's eternal visionary perspective, can man begin to rise and come into the light. Once man could *see* this degradation, he might rise and know the light. "Humility," Edwards said near the end of the sermon, "is a great ingredient of true faith"; and again: "Faith is a sensibleness of what is real in the work of redemption. . . . It is necessary in order to saving faith, that man should be emptied of himself, that he should be sensible that he is 'wretched, and miserable, and poor, and blind, and naked.'" [18] From His side God acts through the immediate, daily world to effect some change which He has willed in our life. Edwards had located the salvation process in the soundest reasoning of the new thought of his day, all the while he was keeping the argument within the best accepted decisions of Christian theology. Yet a paradox at once arose: if man can in no wise initiate his own knowing and salvation, then how can man have a will and be aware of the route his consciousness is following? How can redemption be at all praiseworthy and man a moral being in a presumably moral universe if every act of his body and every motion of his soul is predetermined?

The answer was not in the prior disposition of the world, of the sensible impression, or even of the idea which comes into the mind; to be sure, man cannot be condemned for his "dependence" if he has no power to change his place in the world or modify even his thought. Edwards temporarily answered the paradox by stressing — and this was his new contribution to Christian apologetics — the "afterward," or the history which occurs after the sense impulse has been felt and the impression has been made on the mind. The history of one's self-consciousness is the narrative of redemption.

Edwards's remorseless insistence on the sovereignty of God was, therefore, requisite to that first stage in Lockean, sensationalist epistemology: we "know" because knowing preceded us; God is the origin of the first impression, all impressions, and every idea. Without that beginning, no sense datum or idea could ever be. God's sovereignty was also Edwards's return to the valid experience of sinful man in a day when sin had become a word no longer effective in daily living. For Edwards, sin was as much a content of experience and consciousness as the mind itself; indeed, it was one whole dimension of the mind — that side which responded weakly, helplessly, or wrongly to the instant impulse or to the lifetime's direction. Thus sin was not doing but being; and man's admission of his infinite triviality in the presence of God's eternal sovereignty was the first hesitant step toward self-knowledge and redemption. And redemption was a process which ever began inwardly and ever continued within the most secluded domain of human consciousness. It was a lonely way, but man had what he was given and he had the possibility of becoming, and they were enough.

3

The Covenant and God's Incentives

IT IS one of the anomalies of his thought and preaching that Edwards should have resisted the doctrine of God's sovereignty, that he should have felt an almost oppressive cloud darkening his spirit as he struggled with it in the days of his youth, and that he then returned to it in the earliest days of his ministry. The doctrine of God's sovereignty was both a theological principle and a private point of view: it was a true principle because it showed man as he is — trivial, degraded, yet capable of being lifted up; and it served a young man's search for understanding because it put him so low that he could be restored only by an act of God's grace. By 1731 Edwards had not, of a certainty, gained a full assurance of his state of being; he would never have that pride of heart which is the danger to the believing Christian. Yet, in the earliest days of his ministry in Northampton, he had to face the question of God's sovereignty in ways which he had not hitherto considered. He seems to have discovered that, as he reinstituted the tests for slavation and the inquiry into a believer's state of being, he was returning to and reviving issues which had long ceased to trouble the minds of his parishioners. The central question was the doctrine of the Covenant; it is and, in 1731, it was one of the most troublesome issues in New England thought. That it was dying or quite in abeyance did not make it any the less troublesome; in Edwards's hands the doctrine received its fullest, and finest, treatment; after he had done all he could to make it meaningful, it virtually disappeared — only to be reconsidered in the twentieth century because it is of central importance to the New England mind. To give it a brief statement is to risk the charge of superficiality; yet, because Edwards spent some of his best intellectual effort in defining its terms and in showing how it was the only logical expression of God's purpose in human history, we must seek to present some of its main designs.[1]

1

In the beginning was God. Then, by an act of His will, God created the universe, set it in motion according to His prior intention, and placed man in it. But man, because of his very likeness to God, fell; the fall was not simply man's arrogant, self-willed corruption of himself; it was an historical moment when the whole universe shuddered, and all things, from the smallest atoms to the largest planets in their spheres, were forever damaged. Never again, until by an act of God's restoring grace, would the universe of matter and phenomena be coherent and organized as it had been in the times of its pristine wonder. Men would live in a flawed world with their cloudy, flawed minds seeking to apprehend their little plots on which they lived.

God, because He is a beneficent God, did not forthwith at the Fall leave man hopeless or wreak His righteous anger on the new world He had created but, out of His boundless goodness, instituted with man the Covenant of Works. By the terms of this compact man agreed that he deserved to live, work, and die in a world he by his folly had corrupted; yet by an exercise of a most dutiful obedience to God and by doing everything in his power to make God's way obtain in this wicked world, man might, in some good time, be returned to a partial realization of his godlike being. Good works would not wipe away all of the stain of the evil wrought by man's first parent; nevertheless, in ways which no one could foresee, God might allow to later generations of men a greater wisdom and a better life than He had permitted the immediate children of Adam.

The Covenant of Works, instituted with Adam and maintained with mankind throughout all ages, was not, however, sufficient to bring man back from that dark and fallen state. God, because He is a loving God, could not leave man bereft and outcast forever. In a time which He foresaw even before man had fallen, God would send His Son, who would take upon himself man's base condition and, by undergoing the sufferings, the ignominy, and even the death which is the lot of all mankind, would restore man to a condition more nearly like that which he had enjoyed in the days before Adam's crime. This was the Covenant of Grace, a "new Covenant, a covenant of life," in the words of Ames. For Edwards "Christ at his death made over the blessings of the new covenant to believers, as it were in a will or testament";[2] yet clergymen differed and disputed among themselves: some argued that Christ's atonement, His assumption of man's sin and death, was complete and that thereafter men who believed and received the full benefit of salvation enjoyed a complete restoration of what had been lost with Adam's willful act. Others were not so sure: the atonement may have been only partial or "limited"; the flaw of our first parents went so deep not only in the human soul but throughout the whole world of matter and spirit that not even the Son's sacrifice could restore the flawed universe to its pristine state.

The doctrine of the "new covenant" or Covenant of Grace created such difficulties that the Puritan mind was both tormented and invigorated throughout the whole seventeenth century. It was one of those ideas in the human mind which are by nature insoluble — who can decipher the mind of God and His universe? — but, in all the attention it received and in all the dexterity it demanded, it kept the Puritan conscience bright and the Puritan intelligence awake far longer than any other idea, certainly far longer than an idea which could be resolved. Puritanism "solved" the question of the relationship of man to the state, of the place of the single citizen to the City on the Hill: from Winthrop's Address to the Massachusetts Court of 1645 to Wise's *Vindication of the Government of New England Churches* in 1717 this question was readily answered. But the doctrine of the Covenant of Grace defied all man's best thought.

The nagging problem was not so much the mystery or the revelation of God. It was a double question; the first was that of history; the other was one of the single conscience of man. We might consider them briefly in order.

At times propitious in human history God had revealed Himself to the children of men. One occasion was in the institution of the Covenant of Grace at the time of Christ's birth, life, death, and resurrection; that occasion did not end with Christ's leaving the earth, for God remained in the being and presence of the Holy Spirit as the ministrant to the redeemed among men. Another historical manifestation of the Covenant of Grace was at the time of the dispersal of the Apostles to preach the Word throughout the Mediterranean world; still another was the vision of the New Jerusalem which came to the early Protestant reformers; the last in most recent history was God's promise to His chosen people which had been fulfilled when He led the English dissidents from their homeland across the perilous waters and to the forbidding shores of the New World. The "new-covenant way," as the Puritan called it, was that plan which God had ordained for His children to complete in the last fateful hour of the world's history. And the "company of the Elect" were "the chosen ones among the ruins of the Fall, whom [God] appointed to Felicity in the days of Eternity before the World was." [3]

The question of the Covenant and its place in history was less troublesome than the more imponderable issue of the "company of the Elect": who were they? Quite obviously, the saints even before the coming of Christ — Moses, Isaiah, and the prophets — had been granted some special knowledge of God; and surely the "saints" among the first-generation migrants to New England had been numbered in that sacred company; and just as surely, as the energy of that movement had waned and the colony had been blessed with rich increase and the profits of men's handi-work, the roster of names had been depleted in these latter and sorrier generations. If God had chosen the company of the elect even before the Fall (He had forecast that event), then, in this world of confusion and suffering, how could any man know who was in that company? What were the signs, what were the tests and proofs of salvation or damnation? Some among the Puritans declared that the marks of God's election were unmistakable — a holy manner, a holy life, a deep inward conviction. Others averred that the proofs were in self-sacrificing devotion to the serv-ice of one's fellow men. This answer was most problematical and dangerous of all, for it confused the Covenant of Grace, the new covenant, with the old covenant, the Covenant of Works. If the Covenant of Works merely rephrased the terms of the Covenant of Grace, then man need only do what he considered his best, and God would reward him with eternal life. Man could thereby dictate to God the terms of salvation; should God ever allow such countermanding of His eternal will, then He is no longer God.

Perhaps the generally accepted answer to this difficulty was that of the Reverend Increase Mather, who expressed the thought of a century. God had, in this His last historical intervention, brought His people across the ocean and into the holy way He intended them to follow; but He in no wise granted them all alike the state of election. If the company of the elect should always be few, its strength would necessarily be augmented by all the citizens in the holy commonwealth. Thus even damned souls serve God's pur-poses: they work for the general good when, in an inimical and beguiling land, every hand is needed at the hammer to build the homes and churches and at the plow to grow the food that all men may live. Those people who are not elect do not, however, obtain grace by association, nor do they earn it by their labors;

they are simply a part of the community which has been favored by God to accomplish the redemption of mankind in the final hour of history. The company of the elect is quite another citizenship; it is constituted of those whom God, even "before the world was," had named and whom, in His redemptive foresight, He sent His Son to redeem. Man must ever be reminded that God cannot go counter to His prescribed will.

2

By the opening of the eighteenth century, many clergymen, despairing of ever solving the dilemma or simply tiring of the intellectual energy the doctrine required even for its exposition, were plainly declaring that the Covenant of Grace was a tedious argument in dogmatic theology. The Reverend Simon Bradstreet, when he was ordained as minister at Charleston, announced "that he doth not find that God requires persons to enter into a covenant with a particular church," for, indeed, the Covenant has no Scriptural warrant.[4] And the Reverend Solomon Stoddard, Edwards's own grandfather, professed throughout his ministry that men need not be within the Covenant in order to partake of Holy Communion; that sacred offering was, Stoddard declared, available to the saved and to the unsaved alike.

The doctrine of the Covenant subsided not because it was untrue but because it was inapplicable to the lives of men. Puritans, like men of any time, lived not by abstractions or doctrines but by the necessities of their days on this earth, by the unspoken and even unheard declarations of their common will, and by the sturdy and unheroic endurance which made their lives moral and admirable. A Puritan in the early decades of the eighteenth century — the very time of Edwards's ministry — was one of the world's most honest men; he knew that God's signs were undecipherable and that for him to convince himself that he was saved and his fellows were damned was to invite the subtlest working of Satan's guile. His spirit was resilient; he could not countenance the spectacle of a damned world when the sun shone fair, the earth yielded rich increase, and his neighbors seemed not wholly vile.

Yet the doctrine of the Covenant, whether of Works or of Grace, had other adventures in the Puritan mind. While Puritans may be rightly said to have lost their terror of the unseen and with facile ease to have adjusted their lives to the daily necessities of this world, they were, like men of all times and places, faced

with an insufferable moral egotism. They made their principles of religion and their idea of God accord so well with their
common, prudential values that, in spite of some of the most
eloquent warnings of their clergy, they virtually rewrote the
terms of the Covenant to suit their own purposes. Men do not,
however, change readily from one point of view to another; they
reason and debate among themselves; they make flexible and vital
the otherwise rigid dogmas of their teachers. So it was with the
Covenant: it came under scrutiny, and it was modified by the
challenge of several other ideas which rose, all unbidden, to color
and vary what had once seemed an unassailable doctrine. One of
these was the theory of Means and Ends. As the seventeenth
century drew to a close and the eighteenth century opened, men
in New England were reasoning along such lines as these:

The universe of matter has its "covenant," for at creation God
so designed His universe that every atom, every moving body,
and every starry sphere conforms to the predestined end of God's
eternal purpose. There is, wrote the Reverend Samuel Willard,
the ablest proponent of the doctrine, a "necessarily requisite *Sutableness* between the *Mean* and the *End*, Else Means are vain." [5]
The argument is very old in human thought; it is also circular and
self-defeating. If means serve ends, then just those means must
have been intended in order to reach those ends which they were
destined to serve. Similarly, if ends are served by means, then just
those ends inhere in just those means which brought them about.
God's being and His providence can be proved by reasoning
either from means to ends or, contrariwise, from ends to means.

The problem was not one of proving a reasonable and "covenanted" universe, for anyone could see that no atom could move
except as it served aims higher than its mere being. A bird in
flight sings its musical tones which go far beyond the echoing
sound and ultimately merge with the celestial music of the
spheres. The question was basically that of the morality of men:
if man lives his narrow, predestined way and is a means to serve
ends he is powerless to understand, then how can he declare himself a moral being? To be moral he must know not only the
"means" by which he daily lives but the "ends" he eternally
ought to know; if he is but another component of the universe of
means and ends foreordained from the beginning of time, then he
cannot be credited with a moral nature.

The answer was that God's justice, even if it is inscrutable, is
nevertheless "covenanted" justice. Man is not left alone in the

universe; he has his place and he has his duty to perform. Even if the bird is not aware that its song accords with the grander tonality of the universe, it nonetheless performs functions higher and more distinguished than its mere "nature." Man is moral because he does what he must do — and he is granted the gift of reason to know why he does just what he must. Thus the question of means and ends turned, not so much on the destiny and purpose of atoms in motion or the place of man in the universe, but rather on the very practical issue of man's behavior in the world. That issue was, quite simply, one of human happiness. The Reverend Samuel Willard, whose monumental *Compleat Body of Divinity* was a compendium of moral argument for more than half a century, offered the best statement for man's condition in this world: man has a "Nature that he might be Happy, and an Ability to comply with the way of it." [6] This "nature" to be "happy" is God's free gift to all His creatures: the beasts of the field seek their happiness; but the "Ability to comply with the way of it" is a unique endowment of man; it is what makes him a moral being, for by exercising his "compliance" he chooses between kinds and degrees of pleasure and pain, evil and good.

Until Edwards's ministry, Puritan logic was concerned primarily with locating the former history of all ideas and doctrine, not with their manifestation and truth, for their truth was self-evident. The clergy became most artfully skilled, by reason of their training in Ramistic argument, in separating one part from another, origin from development, and first principle from second principle, in the exegesis of Scripture and doctrine. Their sermons, divided into the statement of the text, the extension of the argument, and the application, were devised in order that the true "nature" of the Word of God might be set forth cogently in the lives of ordinary men. The sermon was intended to get behind the factitious and illusory and reach toward the core of thought, the nexus around which the doctrine and its Biblical statement turned.

Truth was, however, not all of a piece; it might be an unquestioned *ens* in the mind of God, but for man on this earth there were as many truths as there were human beings professing the truth. Truth might exist in human minds, but its verification must ever be the prey of the way in which it is stated. Accordingly, Puritan clergymen exercised great dexterity in separating the statement of truth from the "nature" of what is true. A sentence or a proposition can never be wholly and finally true: words are connivances of the intellect and betray the fallibility of their source. A statement like "There is no God" is patently untrue because it denies the being of God at the instant it supposes His existence in the word "God." On the other hand, "Man is an intelligent being" is a proposition which is both true and false: it is false in that it supposes that man has an intelligence which not every human being demonstrates. When, however, one says "Man is," he has a true statement because man has a "nature" which is his present condition; but when one says something about man's "intelligent being," he must support the statement by recourse to the "nature" of the intelligence which his being assumes. Thus to say that "Man is an intelligent being" is to speak a half-truth because one part of the statement relates to the known nature of man and the other part concerns the intelligence of man which the first part in no wise supports. Adequately to prove the truth of the statement would require that one uncover the truth of the two "natures" — that of the man himself and that of his intelligence.

The difficulty of this kind of argument, especially for a modern reader, is that it rests wholly on verbal analysis. The truth or falsehood of a proposition depends, not on the demonstrable evidences of the statement in the world of fact, but on certain prior conditions of the "nature" of logic and thought of which any statement is a verbal analogue; and the ultimate "nature" of any fact or principle lay only in its scriptural demarcation. It is little wonder that Puritan clergymen became skilled in ransacking the Bible for the most remote or appropriate verbal support: God's "nature" is the only true and infinite being; thus God's word is the only true representation of that "nature" and being to man.

Man's reason, albeit a fallible one, is the only portion of His "nature" which God shares with men; yet that reason is not an adequate truth-finding power. If it were, then man would have found the truth a long time ago. Reason is but one of a number of faculties and powers which, since the Fall, have been bestowed on man; the world's increasing burden of sin cannot be attributed to the widening power of Satan nor to the corrupt state of society. Thus John Taylor, one of Edwards's adversaries in this dispute over man's nature and will, could write in his *Doctrine of Original Sin* that "it is not a Man's Reason, separately considered, that produceth the wicked Action; but it is his sinful Propensities, his indulged Passions and Appetites, which have got the Possession and Government of him." [7]

The idea of "nature" and the means-ends argument really were one, for they both supposed that the very flaws in the universe accorded with God's being and purpose. No minor fault, not even the large sin of Adam, could deflect the course of history as God had envisioned it. The commission of sin does not diminish the world's store of good and of happiness; the single act of sin, however it may spell the damnation of the sinner, could never imply that God's nature and plan are called in question. And even as God allows human reason to go counter to His purposes, no despicable act can reduce God's power or lessen the measure of happiness He grants to those who serve Him. An evil act is an impetus for a new and wise course for human reason to follow; the small sin brings a small good, the great sin may even, in time, bring in its train an unseen, an inevitable, and an even greater good. The eloquent Chauncy, who opposed Edwards during the Awakening, realized that evil is not necessarily "evil," for even Satan is a means for achieving the ultimate ends of God. Evil was, according to Chauncy, only a degradation or misapprehension of the good, or what he called "the degeneracy of the powers destined for *good*." [8]

The means-ends argument also answered the problem of conversion. The moment of God's intervention in a man's life was not really a miracle or even a single mediatorial instant: it was an occasion conjoined with the motions of the smallest atom or the circuits of the largest planets in space. Salvation was a dimension of the master-plan which God had instituted from the beginning of His universe. If God acted suddenly and sent a star shooting across the sky, His children need not wonder or be fearful; in good time they would understand. Even the heathen fitted God's ends, for they served the temporal requirements of keeping their part of the world in operation until such a time as the faithful should arrive and take it over.

Almost as though by a stroke of divine intuition, the Puritan doctrine of the Covenant had been joined with the eighteenth-century means-ends argument. The provisions of the Covenant, whereby God from His side inclined toward those men who served Him, were leagued with the observed empirical fact that the better men served the ends for which they were created, the better they prospered in this world. Surely, as Franklin would show, God would hardly reward those in this world whom He intended to condemn in the next, else divine means are a trick and God's ends are a chimera. The more God's and nature's means are served, the better the divine will and nature's laws effect in this world that divine and natural concord which God intends for His children. Even if man's knowledge of God and of this world is only partial and no man can so much as count the hairs on his head, yet, by observing the ordinances of the deity as they are revealed in Scripture and in nature, that second book, man exercises his "Ability" and gains the right to ever greater happiness and the pleasures of God's beneficence. God is a benevolent deity who, as Chauncy effectively stated the principle in the days of Edwards, "would not have left creatures of his forming to such *immoral* conduct as would reflect dishonor on his goodness, by bringing unhappiness and misery into a world of his contriving and making." [9]

The greatest danger in this reasoning was not that it was circular or that it convinced men that the world was created for their pleasure and benefit or that it finally brought about the disintegration of the Covenant — why should the Covenant even exist if the means-ends argument is valid? — but that it left the world split between the objects of the senses and the ideas in the mind, between an invariable causation and the variable understandings which men are permitted to have. If nature is truly moral, it is so under the jurisdiction of God's immutable "laws of nature"; thus no law can go counter to God's prior willing. Even sin is turned to God's ends; the greater the craft and guile of Satan in this world, the more it redounds to God's glory, for God has ordained that everything moves to His inscrutable but well-defined ends.

Another outcome of the principle of means and ends was that laws of nature were lifted to a place equal with and then eventually superior to the Word. In those long-ago times of magic and miracle God had sent the rains to flood the earth, made the sun stand still, and caused the walls of Jericho to fall down because of His direct action. Once men had need of miracle because they were too much benighted in superstition and ignorance; with the gradual elimination of superstition, God had seen fit to let man know Him through the grand symmetrical motions of the planets and the stars, the changing seasons, and the happier content of man's own pride in his wisdom. As centuries passed, however, God's direct interference in His universe had steadily lessened; indeed, it was doubtful if God would ever reveal Himself again. Natural law became, therefore, the latter-day equivalent of antiquity's miracle. When the Reverend Cotton Mather wrote his scientific treatise on comets, readers were refreshed because Mather had set forth the true occasions wherein men may know God through His works. Even the *Remarkable Providences*, that record of extraordinary signs during the witchcraft tirals, was actually objected to by the latitudinarians, who, of all people, wished to maintain some hold on miracle against the steady encroachments of natural science.

Doubtless the fullest and immeasurable result of the idea of means and ends was that the Puritan, certainly by the time Edwards was assuming the Northampton pastorate, was fast losing or had already lost his sense of miracle and of his own most private place in a strange and wonderful world; where once he had eagerly sought that instant chiaroscuro of God's presence in the leaf or sun ray, he now looked indifferently at the nearest object or scanned with aplomb the farthest heavens, sure within himself that God's truth as first cause was everywhere and that all he had to do was to read aright and learn the moral, the second cause. The Puritan risked that greatest of human failings — an insufferable moral egotism; and if he replaced fear and superstition with the leadings of the enlightenment, if he no longer hanged witches, and if he effectively worked for the betterment of his brethren in this world (laudable ideas and actions they are), he nonetheless deprived himself of what had a century earlier given his life its meaning and fulfillment. By 1730 the average Puritan in New England no longer suffered the pangs of an uneasy conscience: like the self-enclosed citizen of the twentieth century, he had assured himself that conscience was a mere relic of bygone days of superstition; in doing so he gained all the prudential values and lost his soul. And very like his children more than two centuries later, he looked upon the world about him with pleasure, with efficiency, with greed, and he began that remorseless destruction of God's place he had been given to inhabit and to till. He might not know it, but his children long afterward would discover it: when men cease to look inward for the truths they must make true for themselves and when they find their world in point-for-point agreement with their every desire, then they may very well be lost beyond recovery.

Edwards set out to counter this errant principle of means and ends with all the logic and eloquence he could muster. That few in his own day heeded him is only an admission that any age ignores its own best thought and lives comfortably, albeit foolishly, within its dark ambiguities and confusions. Yet Edwards's reasoning comes back to haunt us, for it speaks to those unbidden voices men hear in the privacy of their hearts and souls.

3

A Divine and Supernatural Light, that noteworthy sermon of Edwards preached and printed in 1734, was an attempt to counter this insidious and overwhelmingly popular idea of means and ends. The very title would be cause for dismay: light is "light," to be sure, but why call it "divine and supernatural"? Is there any reason for distinguishing that kind of light from "natural" light which shines so beneficently on the earth? The answer is, of necessity, yes, if one believes in and lives by a God not created in man's image.

The effectiveness of Edwards's argument, however much it may have been lost on his contemporaries, was that it took the very basis for the argument for means, for man's happily reasonable interpretation of the world, and used that argument to support the truth of the contrary idea. "Means" came quite easily from a misapprehension of Newton's laws of motion and Locke's theory of the mind. Newton was the last man to propose a machine universe whose every part subserves the pleasure and benefit of man; indeed, Newton's theory had presumed, as we have seen, that so-called "laws of nature" are mere verbal approximations to what man appears to find; laws of nature are not immutable, and the future generations may find so many gaps and flaws in the grand design of a clock universe that the only reality may be, after all, the cogent idea, not the fact. And Locke's theory of the mind, while it seemed to fashion a coherent equation between things in nature and ideas in the mind, had actually proposed something quite different: since words are not real but are mere fictions, cloudy images of what the mind sees, then the ideas in the mind are not in any sense of the word "ideas": they are those necessary apprehensions by which men endure and prosper; they may have no irrefutable validity or reality. Into this gap between the objectivity of things and the tantalizingly questionable ideas in the mind, both Hume and Edwards moved with devastating logic. Hume showed in a paragraph of extraordinary brilliance in the *Treatise Concerning Human Understanding* that objects are in nature and ideas are in the mind because we want and we need to have them there in just those relations in which we see them. The mere fact that we want and see them is no reason to trust their existence or truth.[10]

Edwards reasoned, not by a theory of the mind, but on a principle of being, on ontology. It was to no purpose to reason from the mind or to trace from the mind's ideas back to the objects in nature by means of the supposition that the connections along the way are logical and true. It was to no purpose, furthermore, because the mind is not simply a "mind" situated at the top of a human being's consciousness: what the mind is depends wholly on what the human being is; his every gesture, motion, response, and thought are part of the "mind," as Edwards had recognized in his not so long ago youth. The mind exists in some immediate, intricate context with everything that has happened, is happening, and will happen. To credit one part of man's being to the necessity of "ends" and another part to the phenomenal activity of "means" is to reduce thinking to nonsense. Thinking and thought are what human consciousness is doing every instant. Even before one was alive, thinking was going on, and long after one has left this world, thought proceeds.

Yet Edwards could not abandon the argument which he sought to undermine. Rather he assumed that it was, if not true, at least relevant, and thus he turned it back upon itself. If thinking and belief are caused, he proposed, then how are physical, sensory causes linked with mental, spiritual, even divine effects? How do thought and conviction transcend mere sense experience, that "ghastly hold of reality"?

In committing himself partially to the logic of dual causation, Edwards proposed that knowledge or grace is twofold; it is common and it is supernatural. By common perception Edwards meant that which we share in common in daily living and experience. Yet as we share the world, we do so with striking differences one from another: we have from birth a curious dissimilarity, a tendency which makes each one go a way different from all others. This tendency cannot be in nature, for nature, even to be nature, is coherence, regularity, and predictableness. The difference must be in human consciousness itself; and here Edwards took his reasoning back to what he had considered in "Notes on the Mind." Our sharing the world in common is not dependent on the commonness of the world; it is not the air, the light, the objects of our vision which are common, for they are in nature and do not belong to us. Rather it is a "grace" which we share in common; and "grace" can be considered, at least on this level, as the tendency and the possibility man has for overcoming his baseness; it is what "assists the faculties of the soul," in Edwards's words, "to do that more fully which they do by nature." [11] When he spoke of "nature," Edwards did not mean that essence of man behind all appearance or that natural being which he shares with all members of the human family; by nature Edwards meant the defective part which was forever left from Adam's sin. Our "nature" is what thwarts and belittles us; "grace" is what offers to lift us up.

The tendency toward and the power of knowledge are, therefore, not in nature, for nature or the world of daily experience is riven by the great flaw which has forever put an affront upon nature. The beggarly elements intrude and beguile. What Edwards was seeking was a principle whereby nature, even flawed by man's first and continuing crime, could nonetheless be regarded, even as Locke's thought had proposed, as the beginning of grace and understanding. God could not have allowed His world to degenerate entirely; to be His world it still must function according to laws more enlightened than mere motion, cause, and effect. In this sermon of 1734 Edwards presented his early objective idealism in its most eloquent and attractive form.

The effects of the world on the senses begin, of necessity, in a first cause and continue with unbroken regularity throughout the whole course of time. Yet Edwards was not able, by reason of the dominating thought of his time, to make "first cause" a simple, invariable causation such as would end in merely brute determinism. "First cause" had, throughout the course of centuries, been variable: each age had built on the lessons of its ancestors, and the centuries moved in their long procession from the fables of old to the natural laws of the present. Galileo's stars and Newton's atoms appeared to move with an invariable precision; the very knowledge of stars and atoms suggested that, if first cause were a rule of the universe, it was not a law of the human mind. What the Greeks had known far surpassed the knowledge of the Egyptians, and what men of the eighteenth century possessed, though it might make them vaunt themselves unduly, exceeded anything that seers had dreamed of old. If natural law obeyed first cause and matter went the route predetermined by all the forces of the world, then human thought, albeit it derived its first awareness from nature, can go its own way and even be, perhaps, capricious. Man in this latter time has come to know things he had never known before; he has been permitted a new and greater understanding, not because first cause and natural law are invariable, but because God, by His working through the world, has but recently disposed what is to be known. "Men by mere principles of nature," Edwards wrote, "are capable of being affected with things that have a special relation" to their minds and souls. The relation is "special"; it is not invariable.[12]

Edwards was concerned not with psychology but with ontology; he needed to answer the question: Why is it that cause is not always uniform in human life and thought? He reasoned that "cause" is dual: there is a rule of causation for atoms in motion and another rule for minds in the act of thinking. By means of terms more appropriate to his day than to ours, he called them "common" and "supernatural." Even God's first cause had itself a causation, a beginning, and it has had differing manifestations throughout the centuries of men. Thus first cause is the ostensible givenness of things; it does not pertain to or account for the infinite disparity in human sensing and knowing. For if first cause be all we have, then we are poor and deprived indeed. Edwards reasoned, therefore, on the well-known Puritan idea of second cause or of "supernatural" force; it forms that domain of experience which man can inhabit and know quite apart from his sensory perception of things. This domain Edwards variously named; on this occasion of *A Divine and Supernatural Light* it was "excellency" — that which excels and surpasses all other things.

Edwards needed to demonstrate that knowing in no way depends on mere sense experience. "The Spirit of God acts in a very different manner in the one case," he wrote in his ministerial manner, "from what he doth in the other."[13] Take, for example, the idea of time. We say that time passes, that it moves, and that it hurts or soothes. Yet time is not a series of consecutive impressions on the mind, like drops of water falling on the head. Time does not inhere in the sunrise or in the linear movement of the day; yet men live by time with as clear necessity as they rely on food and light. Thus time is a content of men's lives and consciousness and is, to some extent, recognizably the same in all men — they will agree that a day contains twenty-four hours — and yet is as different as the faces and behavior of different men. Time is accordingly somehow devised within the mind itself; it is the aggregate of infinite numbers of impressions which are so arrayed that they seem to have sequence and coherence. Yet they only "seem," for the instants of perception are not joined in nature: the rays of light which this moment come from the sun and enter the open eye are not unified; indeed, according to Newton's theory of light and Edwards's own youthful experiments, light is the most fragmented of particles and of sensation.

"Excellency" is therefore the character and power of the mind to sense and to know according to its own route and cause (a "second cause") which, while it is leagued with every motion in the outer world, is all the while impelled from within. The being of man is self-contained and potentially self-fulfilling. It is not a prey and victim to every circumstance but is guided by "a divine and supernatural light." Edwards defined this light or excellency in narrower terms, but they suffice: "And it may be thus described: A true sense of the divine excellency of the things revealed in the word of God, and a conviction of the truth and reality of them thence arising." Edwards insisted that this sense of excellency was not unique or privative, it is "twofold." At its most common and prudential level it is the agreement that one is bound to his material being, to his senses, and to those "notions" which are the impulses and acts of his daily living. On the other level it is "that which consists in the sense" or the feelings "of the heart: As when . . . the heart is sensible of pleasure and delight in the presence of the idea of it. In the former is exercised merely the speculative faculty, or the understanding, . . . in distinction from the will or disposition of the soul. In the latter, the will, or inclination, or heart, is mainly concerned." [14]

However man may be a "twofold" being and subject to the primary and secondary laws of the world and of his own being, Edwards had in 1734 declared that a man, any man, is a whole and an incalculably complex being. Experience is not the units and particles of existence, divided between the needs of the flesh, the ideas in the mind, and the perceptions of the spirit: experience is all that the body senses and the mind knows even when knowledge is incomplete and sensation is deceptive. Feeling becomes thought; the character of the sensation molds the shape of thinking; and what a man thinks is very likely the way he feels. Even the grandest moments of one's life are lived through and known by means of their webbing and filiation with the texture of the world all around. And thought or the mind is empowered to live both outwardly in its sensations and inwardly upon itself: the ideas of time, of truth, of God, of eternity are not subject to the measure of atoms and the spaces of the stars. They are the ultimate reach of the human mind when, from its sensory notions through that intangible line of "second cause" to the "spiritual and divine light" available to men who will seek it, everything

comes to have "an excellency that is of a vastly higher kind, and
more sublime nature than in other things; a glory greatly distinguishing them from all that is earthly and temporal." [15]

Thus for Edwards, first and second cause are both "cause";
they are elements together in the illimitable structure of God's
universe; they are known by men, not as fragments and laws, but
as everything that makes up living, thinking, and believing. Just as
Locke had traced the route of sense impressions which become
ideas, Edwards sought the way by which that "common good"
we all share in this world as children of Adam becomes "inherent
good" or what in *A Divine and Supernatural Light* he called
"excellency." The question was, therefore: Are the activity and
thought of the soul in man as confined to its range as is the mind?
Does "inherent good" so bind the spirit that it must receive just
those incentives and have just that direction which the predeter-
mining will of God has ordained? The answer is, of necessity, It
does: the soul has no more power of thought than the body has
control over its motions or the mind can affect its ideas: "the
inherent good is that excellency or pleasure which is in the soul
itself." [16]

A decade earlier, in his diary for February, 1725, Edwards had
resolved to have "as clear a knowledge of the manner of God's
exerting himself, with respect to Spirits and Mind, as I have, of
his operations concerning Matter and Bodies." [17] By 1735 Edwards was beginning to question or even deny one of his most
fundamental convictions. He was no longer quite so sure as he
once had been in those days of gracious indwellings of the spirit
that what the world offered as the excitement, charm, and wonder of sense response was really a "good." He might call it in *God
Glorified* an "objective" or common good, but by so much as
fashioning a distinction, he was consigning it to a scale of human
response and cognition lower than he had ever considered it before. Physical objects and the sensings of the body marked that
domain of deception, of estrangement, of sin — not because the
world is evil, but because, by being a sinful creature, man is disen-
franchised from living in and perceiving the world aright. The
stone forever releases the power, in Locke's terms, by which it
can be known; but the after-history of that power as the primal
energy flows along the ways of sensing and thinking may become
wholly corrupted. Nature is, of a certainty, flawed, but so too is
man. Edwards was coming to realize, albeit he hardly dared admit
it to himself, what poets and sensitive men come to understand,

that the cheating knavery of the senses and of that shimmering or lumpishly brute world is no place for the activity of the mind or soul. Edwards was beginning to see that truly to build a world within and to discover the character of life God intended each man to have was not to absent oneself from those responsibilities which the world entails — certainly a minister of Northampton could not withdraw from what he was meant to do — but to see those responsibilities as occasions, surmises of the moment, the fleeting necessity which had once seemed to him beautiful but which now was beginning to pall. The circle of his fate was closing slowly about Edwards: it was not the enclosure which lessens a man's power and sensitivity but rather it was the narrowing ring of consciousness itself. Edwards was beginning to pay the penalty of any man who has for a time lived in the wonder and even ecstasy of his senses; not only was he suffering from that irreparable diminution of sensory response which is every man's portion but he was discovering that even what the world had released to him and what his mind had once taken delight in might well have been a delusion.

It was not the delusion of daily living: impulses from the clear or cloudy arena of God's world were forever the same. It was the trickery of one's mind which, by virtue of its being a mind, could follow its own logic and, all unknowingly, condemn itself either to an enslavement to the world or to a self-created solipsism whereby the mind could invent anything it wanted. A solipsistic view is not, even for a Puritan, necessarily evil or even obscuring: one must build his world from within, for God enjoins upon all His children the requirement that they come to Him only as they are in all their sin and their uniqueness. The difficulty with seeing the universe wholly from within one's own private being was that such a view might destroy that fitting and inevitable interchange which God has required of any man who believes and knows. God is, of a certainty, there in the physical and in the phenomenal universe; every instant of His time is a moment of necessary wakefulness. Yet if any man close the valves of his attention (the phrase is Emily Dickinson's), he is in mortal danger of condemning himself to that outcast condition which is damnation indeed. Truly to be a child of God is to be ever receptive to the merest vagary of feeling which may come from God's universe; to withdraw and live within oneself is an awful risk.

Puritans may have suffered from this disease of the spirit without knowing it. Cotton Mather reduced his days of fasting and prayer — those hours of necessary self-scrutiny — to mechanical self-indulgence wherein he pondered, hour after hour, only the visionary perspective he saw within himself. The less he was induced to feel the world as it actually was, the more he turned it into a mechanism of the mind — an infinite analogue which could be read every instant. The winding road through the forest or the door of a barn swinging in the wind was translated into an anagram of the soul; and the soul, seated at the center of one's own being, could look out and know that, as Mather himself proclaimed in the *Essays to Do Good*, everything is divine and very good.

Yet Puritans were not the only victims of this disease of the spirit which goes by various names: the arrogant ambition of men, the principle of the world made for man's joy, or the argument which in the eighteenth century went by the name of Means and Ends. Whatever its name, it has had a long and even noble history. It is even the modern heresy; Hawthorne called it the Unpardonable Sin. By its terms man creates a self-enclosed, self-defining circle of thought and action and then consigns the deity to take care of those untidy corners of existence which man's consciousness would prefer to ignore. Those corners may be anywhere — in the farthest space where only mystery seems to lurk, around the corner of one's village or town where poverty exists, or in the human heart itself which sees itself only as the peak and apogee of all that is. To live within such a circle is to live most comfortably, most elegantly; it is, to be sure, to live a lie. In time the fallacy takes a terrible toll, for eventually a man may come to realize that he is the victim of his own supreme fiction: if he is the master of his private, visionary world, he may very well be his own arch-fiend. Nothing quite so annihilates one's self-esteem as does the specter of the obscene fiendishness of one's self.

By returning to the full and awful demands of the Covenant, Edwards no doubt revived a dying or a dead system of thought. Yet, since no principle ever finally dies but becomes modified amid the daily exigencies of man's life on this earth, Edwards was simply arguing a point very close to Hume's reasoning at about the same time. To be sure, Hume was quite indifferent to a doctrine which was still being preached with more fervor in Scotland than it was even in faraway New England; nevertheless, the idea was the same. It was that human thought depends on incentives, desires, impulses, wishes. Thinking is not the power and the mastery of the mind over that which it knows; rather, thinking is what in order to survive the mind is required to be doing every moment it lives. If Hume were concerned with tracing the thinking of the mind to those antecedent needs which make it think, Edwards was finding in the Covenant of God the rationale for all thought. Man can think, not because he has been given a power called thought; he thinks because God has allowed him a peculiar aptitude for knowing. Just why God should have given him this power is a mystery. It is enough that man has a "nature" to think; it is even more to God's glory that man can think contrary to God's divine ordinances. Thus by his thought man is humbled in order that, perhaps, he may rise again.

4

The World as History

THE Great Awakening, that extraordinary religious event in the history of the colonies, has been the object of almost as much attention as that other remarkable occurrence in American history, the witchcraft delusion of the 1690's. Both are linkd, at least by the uncritical, in the same historical perspective: they were outbursts of errant, uncontrolled "superstition" from which, happily, a wiser and gentler spirit of the people rescued even the benighted. That the witchcraft trials have attracted novelists, poets, and dramatists is cause for wonder, for, aside from the rantings of old women and the confessions of children, the event had very little significance. The Great Awakening, on the other hand, did have drama: it effected a turn in American religious history, for it certainly doomed an already dying Puritanism, and it gave aid to the growing Methodist challenge and indirect support to Unitarianism. That nineteenth-century Protestantism turned "liberal," sectarian, and secular was probably the result of that series of revivals which, however diverse they were, tended to convince men that they were children of God and inheritors of a Kingdom of Heaven, if not of this world in its present state, at least in some future state of worldly accomplishment or supernatural triumph.

Our concern is not with the historical narrative of the Great Awakening, whether in its vibrant spiritual direction or in its broader sociological enterprise. Suffice it to say that, quite unexpectedly, a wave of spiritual distress and of a longing for Christ and His salvation appeared in the Connecticut Valley in 1734 and that, for sixteen or eighteen months, it spread throughout the Valley and into the nearby villages and towns. It did not go much farther than that portion of central Massachusetts, and then it waned. During its course it had been ministered to and recorded by Edwards, whose care of the sin-sick souls and whose words to the wavering may have had much to do with the course of the revival. Then, quite as unexpectedly, a similar mood of religious terror and longing appeared in 1740. This time Edwards seems to have been ready: he had known of the remarkable "harvests," five of them in fact, which his grandfather, the Reverend Solomon Stoddard, had reaped during his long pastorate in Northampton. For Edwards this time was another in that sequence of God-ordained events.

Yet on this occasion Edwards was not alone or simply sharing the work of saving souls with the local clergy. He was joined by the eloquent, dynamic Reverend George Whitefield, an Anglican clergyman, who had come from England and, after one misadventure in the southern colonies, was preaching to numbers of people throughout New England.[1] Whitefield's sonorous voice, as Franklin would testify, rolled in great waves over thousands and carried every syllable to the farthest verge of his hearers. However unlike they were — they were as unlike as two men could be, in temperament, in doctrine, in their ministry — Edwards and Whitefield for a short time joined in the great work of salvation which God had appointed them to perform. Their preaching was singularly different: Whitefield's oratorical power, his ability to improvise, and his sense of playing on the moods of his audience drew his thousands who were especially moved by his one simple doctrine: man is a child of God and, however effectively he may condemn himself, an inheritor of the Kingdom of Heaven. God never damns one of His children; to the last moment of their lives they may call out, be heard, and saved. It was a doctrine quite at odds with what Edwards was preaching. Perhaps the effectiveness of the second phase of the Awakening between 1740 and 1742 was owing to the disparate yet simultaneous preaching of these two remarkable men — the one impulsive, generous, eloquent; the other clear-headed, cautious, yet, in his way, no less eloquent.

For Edwards the Awakening — for the present we shall consider the two phases of the movement as one — was an occasion in mid-career when all his earlier thought and belief were sharply brought against a test which was as unexpected as it was devastating. In such early writings as *A Divine and Supernatural Light* (1734) Edwards had proposed that the spirit of God, while it is predisposed to do what it must, is nonetheless a most personal and unique bestowal of divine pleasure on the individual man. Now he came to realize that God's animating grace is a portion of the whole history of the universe: history is not simply "history," the narrative of God's workings with men; it is also the whole antecedent narrative of the causes and courses of the world. Puritans had for more than a century resolved this question by turning history into a narrative of God's unvarying types. "Types" were the rigorous correspondence of human life and history to infallible Biblical precedents. Thus history was a set of representations which fitted an eternal plan by which truth could be recognized according to the "type." For Edwards, however, history did not precisely conform to typology; that is, it could never offer those convenient relevances whereby one might draw lines of moral reference between Abraham, Joseph, Moses, David, Ahab, or Ezekiel; nor was it a divine allegory which filled the gaps in the continuity of human consciousness. History offered Edwards the full expression of God's grace as that grace had been variously revealed to men; and it was very like the life-history of a single mind which was empowered and required to seek out its own record and to see itself as part of the downfalling and the uprising of the children of men.

Now, however, Edwards had to consider the sociology of incoming grace; not one but hundreds, perhaps thousands, were its potential legatees; if they came to possess grace aright, they would have to be made aware of their possession in terms just as clear as Edwards had made his own private religious life to himself. Furthermore, if religious experience is unique, if the indwelling of God's power is foreordained from the beginning of time, and if the outward physical world bears its own lessons and demands, then the phenomenology of history must be considered: history must move in ways more final than the exigent conversion of just one man. And if the Covenant of Grace is still in effect, as it most assuredly must be, then God may be acting in His history for the consummation of that plan which He set in order nearly six thousand years ago. Edwards was forced, therefore, to broaden his arguments, to look outward from himself, and to find evidences of God's work as vividly disclosed in other people as he had earlier found it in himself. It may be an old story: the thinker and writer who perforce abandons his inner domain of consciousness and enters the busy world of human affairs. If it is an old, it is also a nearly tragic story because Edwards lost his way, not in the bitter rancors of charge and countercharge, but in the reasonings of his own mind. Eventually he had to find his way again back to what he had earlier premised — but that is another, a later narrative.

Edwards tirelessly, remorselessly returned to the Covenant not only as it was coterminous with Locke's theory of the mind on its way through life but as it reaffirmed that man is a moral being every moment he draws a breath, and his morality is founded on the moment's transient vagary and on the lifetime's profoundest conviction. In the course of history, therefore, man's moral constitution has been rejuvenated, first, by direct acts of God such as the dispensations of His grace and, second, by those procedural occasions which, if they seem to have no miracle in them, are nonetheless part of God's purpose for men. By bringing the Covenant into close association with history, Edwards sought to redefine, not God's implacable logic, but man's almost maddeningly various life on this earth. The Covenant does not argue a closed theory of history; that view was the new philosophy of the Cartesians and the Nominalists; for Edwards the Covenant continually, almost effortlessly, opens history and the brightening possibilities for men.

The logic is knotty but important. Edwards would extend and elaborate it throughout his defenses of the Awakening; he would not abandon it even when the Awakening had spent its force and made him return to his former ways of thinking.

2

God's knowledge and God's foresight are conformable to God alone. The Covenant was therefore initiated by God, not by man for man nor by man in accordance with God's prior intentions. If God is good to man, His goodness is not shared with men; goodness is a self-operating principle which belongs only to Him. Yet God did covenant with His people that He would bestow on them more than they could have and more than they deserved to have of themselves. By so agreeing, God became not wholly a free will: He became less than His godhead and thereby ordained that His will would be free only within those self-determining limitations. This self-limiting will shows itself in the "tendency" of nature's laws to do what they are required to do and in the "affections" God manifests to men. God has so limited Himself that the "tendencies" He manifests in the world are restricted to those which man's "affections" are capable of feeling and knowing; God never exerts a force which is not held within the confines of His own will and within the limited range of man's intelligence. " 'Tis also undoubtedly true," Edwards reasoned in the *Treatise Concerning Religious Affection*, "that the Spirit of God is very various in the manner and circumstances of his operations, and that sometimes he operates in a way more secret and gradual, and from smaller beginnings, than at others." God's power is "entirely different from and beyond our power," and, as

Edwards continued in his rather thorny rhetoric, "above the power of nature. . . . Certainly, it is in no wise unreasonable to suppose that this effect" of God's power "should very frequently be produced after such a manner, as to make it very manifest, apparent, and sensible that it is" the power of God and not that of man.[2] God's eternal "tendency" is a power which, even as it seems to act differently in different times, is always the divine law and can never go counter to itself.

Edwards's insistence on the historical continuity of the Covenant — God's "tendencies" are always coordinate with man's "affections," however variously the two may join or separate — was an attempt to maintain the content and validity of single consciousness at the same time that Edwards sought to place the growth of consciousness within its own special moment in history. Man builds his world from within, but what he uses to build that world is provided for him by the data of knowledge and the effects which the history of his time offer him. God's "tendencies" and man's "affections" meet on these two points: man's own being and the world's condition. One of Edwards's most interesting inquiries into this dual placement of man's consciousness is *A History of the Work of Redemption*, originally a series of sermons delivered in Northampton in 1739; it was a time when the first momentum of the Awakening had subsided and before another and even more extraordinary demonstration of God's will would be manifested. The *History* is a narrative of mankind from the Fall to the nearer time of Edwards's own day; it is a very long work, broken by passages of unexpected fervor which read like some of Edwards's warnings to his parishioners; it is colored by the awareness that history, even as it appears to have failed God's high purpose, has yet another adventure leading to its end in the redemption of man. Its central doctrine is "The work of redemption . . . that God carries on from the fall of man to the end of the world";[3] yet, by an unusual application of the historical covenanting of redemption for man, Edwards sought to reveal the doctrine of God's justifying power and also detail the life-history of the single man in quest of self-knowledge. If the *History* reads like the most conventional Puritan typology, it glows with the clear insight Edwards had into the meaning of history to the individual man.

Edwards reasoned that any one of God's actions occurs not once but sustains an all-informing purpose in history. Another way of stating the principle is by means of the antitype and the type: "from the fall of man to our own day," Edwards noted, "the work of redemption and its effect has mainly been carried on by remarkable communications of the spirit of God" which have been an all-informing action, not once, but throughout the whole of history. One occasion is duplicated long afterward; one sign appears time and again for the advantage and the leading of men; history is therefore never complete — or, rather, history is finished at its very beginning, but its disclosure to the murky visions of men is an enlarging perspective, an ever-widening corridor, through time. Thus the Flood was the type of the washing away of sin by means of Christ's sacrifice; the tower of Babel, or "Babylon" as Edwards called it, was a sign of man's arrogant presumption that he could reach to heaven; Abraham was called to journey from his homeland as a presage to God's singling out His chosen people and to His eventual salvation through the death and resurrection of Christ. The events which took place before the Christian dispensations were, in Edwards's validation of history, not merely types or clues to the coming redemption: Christ was actually present in and working through the occasions of history; he was in the cleft of the rock which Moses struck; he was in those divine interventions when the people of Israel were saved from destruction at the hands of their enemies; he was in human form before the seventy elders, and he was a guide to Joshua, who was himself a type of Christ: "Joshua" and "Jesus," Edwards insisted in conformity to the newest philological reasoning, "are the same name." [4] "Christ thus appeared time after time, in the form of that nature he was afterwards to take upon him; because he now appeared on the same design, and to carry on the same work." "The events of providence," Edwards concluded in *A History of the Work of Redemption*, "are not so many distinct, independent works; . . . but rather so many different parts of one work, . . . one regular scheme. God's works of providence are not disunited and jumbled, without connexion or dependence, but are all united, just as the several parts of one building: There are many stones, many pieces of timber, but all are so joined, and fitly framed together, that they make but one building: They have all but one foundation, and are united at last in one top stone." [5]

Edwards saw two kinds of history. One was the working of the secular law in the daily lives of men and in the dispositions of nature; the other was the tendency and manifestation of God's sacred, divine law which is, like the secular law, a force in natural and in human life. Even though both laws are demonstrations of the same law (all law is God's), Edwards reasoned that God has allowed certain parts of His world and certain events in history to go their own way. Men are recalcitrant or alive; certain landscapes are lackluster or inspiriting. History is accordingly not an inevitable and monotonous record of God's invariable will: within the divine program small acts of evil, crimes of unimaginable fiendishness, or events which are anti-history can occur. So too acts of heroism and self-disdain, movements of remarkable energy and effect, and even decades of marvellous witness to God's truth are known. Whatever the declension or ascent of history, the world is moving toward its last hour when, with the decrease of learning, the pall of darkness which comes over the earth, and the persecutions which the faithful must suffer, God will bring to a close the plans He had for His children and at the last raise His "church to consummate glory in heaven."

These two versions of history were not merely phenomenal manifestations of God's hand in His universe for the understandings or confusion of men; they were actual scientific law and thereby conformed to the recent theories of Newton and the investigators. In his *An Humble Attempt to Promote Explicit Agreement and Visible Union in Prayer*, published in 1747 shortly after the close of the Awakening, Edwards noted: "All the changes that are brought to pass in the world, from age to age, are ordered in infinite wisdom in one respect or other to prepare the way for that glorious issue of things, that shall be when truth and righteousness shall finally prevail, and he, whose right it is, shall take the kingdom. All the creatures, in all their operations and motions continually tend to this." Then borrowing that favorite of all metaphors for an empirical-spiritual description of the universe, Edwards continued: "As in a clock, all the motions of the whole system of wheels and movements, tend to the striking of the hammer [*sic*] at the appointed time. All the revolutions and restless motions of the sun and other heavenly bodies, from day to day, from year to year, and from age to age, are continually tending hither. . . ." [6]

The curiosity of this analogy for a universe which never varies is that Edwards saw the hand of God working even through His invariability. For, by an interesting variant on Newtonian probability, Edwards reasoned that God's universe could allow for not the slightest deviation from its inevitable course moving "through those vast successive changes . . . from one age to another" in order to "bring forth this glorious event" of the completion of God's plan. Nevertheless, an invariable universe ever allowed for variation: if the atoms and material bodies of the cosmos proceeded along their route of causation, God acted as an "immediate influence . . . upon things," not capriciously but "according to those constant methods that we call the laws of nature." Laws of nature are, therefore, the working of God in His universe for the benefit and "good purposes" of men. To be sure, laws of nature act for the pleasure and benefit of evil men: the "influence of God continues, to make them obedient to men's will, though wicked." Nevertheless, laws of nature are like the rain which falls on the just and the unjust: they are merely the provisional exercises of His power which, if He brought it only under the command of the faithful, would countermand His eternal justice; and "seeing it is but a little while" before the consummation of the divine plan, God "chooses rather to subject" the laws of nature "to man's wickedness, than to disturb and interrupt the course of nature according to its stated laws." [7]

Thus God may be working in His secret way through the normal courses of nature in order to effect even that which must remain mysterious to the minds of men. God's "tendencies" may, if they can be apprehended, reveal through the laws of nature the normal, unspectacular movement of history to its appointed climax; and the typical, secular law, however commonplace it may seem, may likewise be proceeding along its destined, natural route. "Things that exist now, at this present time," Edwards remarked, "are in themselves no more weighty or important, than like things, and of equal reality, that existed in time past, or are to exist in time to come: Yet it is evident that the consideration of things being present . . . does especially affect human nature." [8]

What Edwards was striving to show in this theory which seems like the most errant tissue of Christian typology and post-Renaissance doom-vision was that the minute, daily events in the life of each man are part of and may be explained by the total record of mankind. Each soul is a moment in the vast panorama of history; man is damned or saved as his history is twined and fibered with all other men who were lost or saved; salvation is a dimension of the natural and the phenomenal worlds. Events in the far past are not, therefore, hidden and mysterious acts of the divine will but are "parts of one work" which God set going in His cosmos at the beginning of chronicled time.

Yet a confusion rests at the center of a dual interpretation of history, one for natural causation and the other for God's divine manifestations. How could God have allowed the history of unregenerate men to go its wasted, infamous way through nearly six thousand years and then, quite as though He were countermanding His own established will, have suddenly provided a propitious moment of mercy to come to the unredeemed of earth? For an answer (and it was a good one) Edwards again had recourse to the Covenant in *A History of the Work of Redemption;* it was a resolution he was to repeat many times throughout the Great Awakening.

When God sought to be reconciled with His children after Adam's fall, He did so because He did not intend that all of mankind should die and be forever lost. Yet this Covenant was made only with the "invisible church" — that community of the elect who would live from the days of the patriarchs until the first note which should sound the approach of Doomsday. Even if throughout the intervening ages there were no actual church, the Covenant would still be in force. Abraham and his seed were privileged to live under its terms, even though they were so early as not to understand and to profit aright from that divine offering. So too the patriarchs, judges, and prophets of the Old Testament were ministers of grace under the Covenant; yet they also lived before God fulfilled His promise in the coming of His Son. In order, therefore, that men in those early centuries might have some of the advantages of salvation which could come only after the redemptive process had been manifest in history by means of the Son's life and death, God had given man His "legal institution" and required of him "legal restitution" and "legal humblings." A "legal institution" and "legal" history are provisional and are manifested only in those periods of time when men are indifferent or content to be outside the Covenant; even Mohammedans, pagans, and the great mass of unredeemed are within this law and this history. God's covenanted law and His truly moral history pertain only to those within the Covenant.[9]

Yet the covenanted and the uncovenanted live in the daily world of fact; they share the benefits and the fruits of this world as well as its diseases and death. The unredeemed live only in the "legal" way; they are bound by the natural laws, their appetites, and even their humanity to the course which their world and history take. The covenanted, on the other hand, are citizens of both "ways" and in both histories; if they live aright, they fulfill twin destinies and constitute, accordingly, the community of God's chosen ones on this earth.

In *A Faithful Narrative of the Surprising Work of God*, in his sermons, and later in the more deeply reasoned apologies for the Awakening, Edwards insisted that the marvellous acts of divine grace in the 1730's and 1740's were every moment foreordained by the terms of the Covenant God had made with His children at Adam's fall. Divine justice is covenanted justice; it is not a prescription to condemn the wicked, for they are, like the heathen peoples of the earth, outside the Covenant. At just those propitious moments in God's time, the two roles, the two versions of history meet and converge: the "legal" and the "covenanted" ways come together, and God determines, just for that portion He will allow, that the Covenant shall be broadened in order to include all men.[10] In his most famous sermon, "Sinners in the Hands of an Angry God," Edwards held out this appeal that "Now God stands ready to pity you." The propitious moment of mercy had come. Once it had passed, mankind would wait a long time.

3

The terms "legal" and "covenanted" were more than parts in a system of logic and more than divisions in an argument of theology. They were, as Edwards came to see them during the decade of the Awakening, elements in the very living of a man's days. The "legal" condition was what man was born with; it was what was provided and accumulated for him throughout the passage of seemingly endless centuries wherein men, even one's ancestors, had fallen or risen, been blind or receptive, prepared the way or darkened the path of one's own life. "Legality" was one's earthly inheritance from the beginning of time to the moment of one's birth; in it one shared with all one's fellows the past, the condition of things, the state of society, and all other practical, limiting, and causative energies which together make up the world of living and life. The legal state was, therefore, the narrative of all that had occurred in the course of ages; since that infinitely diverse record could never be recovered and known, it had to be conceived and understood under certain appropriate principles which men in their time found intelligible and correct. To recover the full course of the earth's historical past would be to write the record of man's "legal" state.

The covenanted state was, of course, a quite different condition and it brought with it a quite different history. What had been "covenanted," Edwards came more and more clearly to see as the Awakening went its several courses, was the record of divine history, of God's foreordained interventions in history; earthly, mundane, natural history went its own insensate, atomic way: what it was to be throughout the passage of time was inherently fixed in the atoms themselves; they ran, if not blindly, at least necessitously according to the route which God had required and which, in a cloudy way, Newton and the scientists had discovered. The covenant as history was, however, typical history: God's eternal antitypes were set in the universe of form, but His types presented His occasions for the admonition and direction of men. Thus, while the types were exemplified in the daily courses of life — in the leaf, the sun ray, the wave — the full disclosure of God's intentions for His children upon earth were in those metaphysical alignments and those deep-lying ideas which come with difficulty, sometimes with suddenness, to the minds of men.

Thus history was for Edwards dual: first, it was the inevitable program of atoms and substances along the "legal" way God had fixed in His universe; men by the millions, even sometimes the whole race of mankind, were set in this necessary journey which, while it might not forward the purpose of God in the world, nonetheless kept the plans of God in operation until such time as He foresaw and enlivened the hearts of a few sanctified men and turned history into new ways. The other form of history was God's alone; only He had initiated it, and only He devised its turns and its lines. Even in those eras when men were insensitive and the world seemed only the clash of atoms, God still held in reserve the day or the decade when he would make His surprising occasion live. The community of the saints, living and dead and even still to be born, comprised the citizenry of this state of being; it was, in terms which William Ames had well defined in his *Marrow of Sacred Divinity* (1636), the "invisible church": even if it had no members on earth, it still existed and continued to maintain God's direction on earth.[11] So too, if a "visible church" remained on earth and exercised awful power, it might not contain the body and soul of a single elected man; and, contrariwise, God might designate two or three who would carry on His work with an amplitude and force which defied the measure of men. The two "histories" converged and became one for those rare, extraordinary times when everything, from insensate atoms to the souls of men, seemed to be all one divine enterprise. Then for that precious time of a day, a month, a year, or a decade, the lives of men were wondrous beyond belief. The Awakening was for Edwards one of these remarkable occasions.

Yet Edwards became an historian of the Awakening at a terrible risk, one which changed his life and brought him to the dark time of the 1750's and a new resolution. That narrative of his misadventure we shall need to detail in its proper place. What is important here is to see that Edwards began with an abstract, a metaphysical premise, and then found himself forced into acrimonious, even disquieting disputes with his fellow clergymen and even with himself. For the first and only time in his life, Edwards's journey of the mind was almost wholly shaped by those external irritants and obstacles which he had dislodged or ignored in his earlier years. This is not to say that Edwards's entry into the marketplace of common ideas was prelude to a tragedy of the mind; nor is it to pose the world against abstract thinking and thereby put all the disfavor on the world; it is to suggest that Edwards was a formal logician who bent his first-rate mind and even his personal life to the exigencies of an occasion in Puritan colonial history during which the world of daily solicitude exacted, as it does from poet and dreamer, an awful penalty. If there were blame to be placed and a fault to be credited, they were Edwards's: he had, almost as though he had foreordained his words and his role, contrived it himself. His gallantry and heroism are implicit in his never flagging in his energies or failing in what he considered his proper calling. To tell that story is not to invite regret at the waste of talent; it is rather to appreciate that some men — a Pascal or an Emerson — willingly made their life's enterprise subserve a time's demand; that they fail is merely to credit the resistant power of the world with an appreciable guile and an ironical habit of going its way. Edwards endured, accordingly, a twofold danger, both aspects of which he faced squarely: one was his passionate conviction that the two "histories" had converged in the times of remarkable harvests of souls, and his need to defend that conviction turned him into what we in our clumsy word would call a sociologist of religious experience; he became an analyst of the intimate concerns of human life on the basis of statistics and apparent demonstration. An historical premise allowed him to conceive that the moment of salvation today is leagued with all moments in the past — and yet that this moment is itself unique. The other danger Edwards faced, a more perilous one, was that he devised a split between nature and thought and, in the end, put an affront upon the world of immediate delight. To be sure, he may already, certainly by 1742, have lost that remarkable sense of feeling and living he had once had; but the ardent defenses of the Awakening turned him from all that light and color and shape had meant to him in his preceding years. Let us consider the idea of history first.

If one reads Edwards's *Narrative of the Surprising Conversions*, the *History of the Work of Redemption*, and other inquiries into the drama of the Awakening, he is early convinced that Edwards's idea of history is an odd fusion of stale Biblical analogies and pious trust that whatever was to be would eventually come to pass in just the way God intended it. Edwards seems to be aware of Biblical scholarship in his day;[12] he knows the relationship of the Septuagint to the rest of Old Testament writing, and that many of the original texts of Scripture were composed in a Hebrew patois and later translated into Greek; he can even rejoice that, by God's willing, Greek most propitiously became the language of learning throughout the Roman world and thus prepared for the wide dissemination of Jewish and Christian thought from the fall of Alexander to the fall of Rome. Yet in almost every respect, from a modern point of view, Edwards's survey of history is worthless if not absurd. He was writing at a time shortly before modern historiography with Vico, Voltaire, and Gibbon was born; and reading every text, whether it is Jacob's dream or the young man Solomon's rhapsody to his love, as if all were equally true puts Edwards far outside the way that history was to follow.

A Faithful Narrative of the Surprising Work of God (1736, 1737) is a treatise on the psychology of conversion. It traces the reasons why the Awakening came with stunning effect to the Connecticut Valley. The people in the villages and on the farms were known for their sturdy piety and attention to religious duties; the two ministers, especially the renowned Stoddard, had reaped five "harvests." Furthermore, the isolation of Northampton and the adjacent towns from the sophisticated centers to the east seemed to promise that even though each locale would have its own conversions, the act of saving grace was quite apparently the working of the Holy Spirit among all the inhabitants together; and even if one town enjoyed salvation on terms different from those of its neighbors, there was nevertheless a marked unanimity of spirit among all the people. Again, Edwards stressed the manifestations of saving grace among the young, especially

among those who were notorious "company keepers" and fre-
quenters of taverns; the sudden and tragic death of a young person in 1734 was the signal for this great change which brought
sobriety, prayerfulness, and a new dedication to those who had
been most scapegrace. Finally, Edwards credited the threat of
Arminianism — the heretical doctrine that man can save himself
and that God stands ever ready to receive the repentant sinner —
with pointing the obvious path to damnation and thereby
bringing the people hard against the prospect that, if the Arminian principle is true, then the Covenant no longer prevails.
Thus Edwards declared that, long before "this effusion of God's
grace" had come, men by the dozens and hundreds had been for
years "concerned about their salvation." God did not startlingly
intrude Himself; He had been negotiating with men and pre-
paring the way and the day for His indwelling grace even while
the citizenry was ignorant and heedless.[13]

By so stressing the antecedence and the "sensibleness" of these
occasions, Edwards might have turned his narrative of the Awakening into one long, tiresome account of the identical workings of
grace in an identical way on all the people. The record is quite
different. Even if God is always the same God, if His power is
unchanging, and if He acts uniformly on His world, the history
of the Awakening, from the story of little Phebe Bartlet to that of
Abigail Hutchinson, is every time a different account. Edwards
endlessly complicated his defense (for it was a "defense" of the
conversions) by arguing from immediate cases and from particular instances in order to present the whole record of God's direction of the people. Indeed, Edwards sought, and found, a new
method of detailing spiritual experience: by abandoning the old
form of the Character, distinguished since the days of Bacon,
Overbury, and Bunyan and sanctified in Cotton Mather's lives of
sixty eminent divines in the *Magnalia*, Edwards entered a murky
way in his search for the particulars of religious experience.

The instants and occasions for incoming grace are countless;
there is no accredited character of the damned or, afterward, of
the saved man, but "a great deal of difference," Edwards said, "as
to persons' distinctness"; or again, "There is a vast difference
. . . in the degree, and also the particular manner of persons'
experiences." [14] Thus the psychology and the phenomenology of
religious life can be conveyed only as religious experience is lived;
and since the one who has lived or is passing through the experience is unaware of what is happening to him and even later can-

not chart all the byways of his soul's passage (even Bunyan had to tell his conversion story twice: once as he imagined it in *The Pilgrim's Progress* and again as he thought it had happened in *Grace Abounding*), Edwards, in order to verify the moments in history, had to reconstruct them, sometimes as they had actually occurred and sometimes as they seemed. In observance of proper historical accuracy, Edwards carefully dated the hour and the moment when the "surprise" and the realization had come, but he was not bound to a mere accurate rendering of what the converted man's fallible memory reported; he was empowered to give the event a clarity of which the converted man was unconscious and to invest the narrative with words of a sort which, owing to the endless diversity of religious experience, most men lack and which only the practiced rhetorician can supply.

Edwards was not, however, telling the story of one or another person's conversion. He was already a master in the art of spiritual autobiography: he had kept his own pulse, he had listened to the heartbeat of his conscience heeding God's word, and he had written his case-narrative of spiritual ebb and flow. In some ways, therefore, the *Narrative of the Surprising Conversions* and other histories of God's remarkable directions for men are versions of Edwards's own spiritual autobiography: what he had lived, suffered, and found ecstatic he discovered was true and valid for the most unbelievably diverse children, women, and men. The private way, the inspiriting hour, and the downfalling of the heart were like the workings of nature: God's laws were everywhere present in the world; He from His side of the veil of reality exerted His force, and men responded according to their characters, their preparations, and the intention God had for them. The very phrases Edwards had employed in his early Resolutions and would later use in his *Personal Narrative* were vivid in the narratives of others' conversions: words were not merely well-worn and tested; rather, Edwards had first found them adequate to his own account and private scripture, and then he made them into the record of those whom he had observed.

It would be easy enough to call Edwards a "poet" of religious travail and joy, and so he was, if by poet we mean a writer who uses quite special, even brilliant, metaphors and symbols as a way of presenting the most inward cases of conscience. In this way Edwards would be a poet like Anne Bradstreet or the more remarkable Edward Taylor; but he was so with his own difference. Puritan poetry, as with Wigglesworth for all his inflamed imagination, was wedded to the invariable types; or, if it broke with the norms of typology, it did so at the risk of triviality or, as sometimes with Taylor, of reverent quibbling, as though a pouting child were talking to God. Edwards's poetic vision (we may rightly call it that) was a way of detailing the psychopathology of religious experience as if it were wholly controlled by metaphors of perceiving of light. What he could "see" he could present in its instant, and variable, configuration; what remained behind the dark vesture of the unseen he had to pass by. Thus the best and most memorable passages in *A Faithful Narrative of the Surprising Work of God* are visions of lonely, suffering, lost men coming quite normally and unexpectedly into the light. It is light "like the dawning of the day"; now it fades and now "it appears again and shines a little brighter"; some in their ecstasy "see a great light dawning" and they know their old life has ended and "all things become new." The Word of Scripture is generally seen, not heard; it breaks in upon the recalcitrant soul: "It seems" to converted men "that the things they see are so plain and easy, and rational, that any body can see them." In another place Edwards notes: "There seems plainly to be an immediate and extraordinary influence, in leading their thoughts to such and such passages of scripture, and exciting them in the memory." And yet "when God withdraws, they find themselves as if [they] were blind again." One of Edwards's most effective defenses of the Awakening is his idea of "pictures": people can have "within them ideas strongly impressed, and as it were lively pictures in the mind." These "pictures" of true visions remain long after the initial effect of God's grace has been felt; and just as the mind can hold in memory the object after it has been seen, so God indelibly impresses on men's minds the lineaments of Himself which He wishes to remain. Even if Edwards had honestly to admit "the difference between what is spiritual, and what is merely imaginary," he never wavered in his conviction that, once God had left an imprint of Himself on man's soul, the human life had been changed.[15]

In the accounts he wrote of others' experience Edwards revived much of his own visionary clarity and vitality which had been for a time lost. What he could see in their lives, he witnessed once again in his own life as he had formerly known and lived it and as he hoped he too might be refreshed. In these records of quite ordinary men and women Edwards rediscovered some of those lines and colors and that light and shade through which he had lived and in which he had brilliantly cast up his own account. Even if some of the *Narrative* smacks of the disputant and the defender of the Awakening, much of it has the poetic freshness of one man's life relived in the vivified lives of others. Dogma so dear to the theologian and the taut logic of the metaphysician fade before the gleaming promise that now this and now that life has been found in the light of encompassing truth.

Edwards's narratives of conversion took the form of a meditative lyric which thrust upward a human soul having the light of God's grace shining upon it. The light never shone the same way or along the same slant twice: it could come to Edwards's uncle, Joseph Hawley, and make him commit suicide under the dread compulsion of Satan; it could also come with quiet serenity to little Phebe Bartlet in her closet and let her know God was near. The light was never "typical" light; it was just that gleam and afterglow which had been bent and refracted to be what it was on that instant or hour of one's coming to know it. Between God and the longing heart intervened the whole physical and phenomenal universe: what Newton had suggested in the *Opticks* Edwards believed he could see working in the souls of men and women. Thus Edwards had to present each person's seeing and knowing the light in quite different ways: and while the narrative of the sinner who enjoyed a "vastation" and then came to the extraordinary assurance of God's presence might follow certain well-determined narrative lines (some of Edwards's accounts do read like the well-known character-study from Bacon to Cotton Mather), the light of God's incoming grace did shine with a difference on different people.

The lyric, meditative quality of Edwards's case-histories in conversion is nowhere better shown than in the best-known of all his records, the narrative of Phebe Bartlet. When she was only four years old, this child heard a voice speaking to her, and she replied: "Pray, blessed Lord, give me salvation! I pray, beg, pardon all my sins!" If her more earthbound sisters chided her for her religious intensity, she broke into tears and could hardly be consoled by her mother calling her by the family pet name, "Nabby" and "Poor Nabby." Her minister, Mr. Edwards, would frequently be in attendance; and when he had been away and was returning, she would speak in "an elevated voice" as if she had heard "the most joyful tidings." Phebe was a child, to be sure, hardly out of her infancy, but she had known the light of God. Modern interpreters might see, not the light of God, but the workings of a powerful delusion in the child's mind from which, if she were to live that sane and healthy life for which our duller century earnestly strives, she was doubtless afterward rescued.[16]

Edwards knew that the workings of God's way with Phebe Bartlet were not merely for that child's joy and salvation; the exercises of God were never fully known by Phebe herself, even if she grew to maturity. The fullest consequences of Phebe's life were in the meditative afterthought of Edwards or of any man who was empowered to record the event. For the event was not fully known until it was recorded; and just as the Old Testament scribes carefully set down the wonders and the punishments of God, so too Edwards wrote a "scripture" of Phebe and all the others who had been enlightened.

Yet Edwards's scripture had a difference: the recorders of the Old Testament and of the New had themselves lived close to or actually in the great events they described; the age of miracle was contemporary. In the long afterward of the world's history God no longer revealed Himself directly; what He showed of Himself He implied through secondary operations of His power and will; "science" might be, though it was doubtful if it were, as clear a revelation of God and His grace as the water which sprang from the rock in the desert or the water which was turned into wine. God had not withdrawn into the farther distances of His universe; He had allowed man a fuller and further exercise of reason which, by God's beneficence, must properly accord with God's own grace.

Reason was not, however, the way to understand the cases of conscience which the Awakening presented. The narrative of the soul's struggle had to be seen, like the miracle of old, at the moment of its greatest travail or joy. But how could one man, Edwards or any other, be present in the quiet hour or in the deepest commitment of the soul to its Maker? Even if, as he often did, Edwards heard the very words and knew the appointed hour of the soul's transformation, he was not truly empowered to write the narrative of these surprising conversions until he had seen them as agreeing at every point with his own struggle, his own ascending spirit, even his own despairing heart. Edwards's narratives were, therefore, solipsistic; they were in that same vocabulary of meditation he had himself used in his private Resolutions and in his journal. It may have been a vocabulary available and common to all writers on religious experience; yet it was also the language of the soul on its journey which Edwards himself, because that journey is never the same, had gone alone. The only way he could narrate the lives of the converted was by seeing them as he had seen and was still seeing himself, even if he had to admit on another occasion that his spirit was not so "lively" as it had once been.

What Edwards recorded was instants of perception which only the language of meditative recollection could capture and hold. It was a very special vocabulary, even though it might contain the words of common discourse; for, if the narrative were told aright, it would conduct the reader or hearer along, not the way Phebe or another person had gone, but along that strange, indefinable way that the reader himself might go. The narrative was a substitute journey, a record of one's own possible quest; its turns and deflections were like those of the light which passed over or around the obstacles in its way and finally reached the eye of the beholder. The effectiveness of Edwards's preaching and writing during the Awakening is nowhere better evident than in his ability to present another's experience as if it were that moment being lived. There is this striking moment in the life of Abigail Hutchinson:

> Once, when she came to me, she told how that at such and such a time she thought she saw as much of God, and had as much joy and pleasure as was possible in this life; and that yet afterwards God discovered himself yet far more abundantly, and she saw the same things that she had seen before, yet more clearly, and in another and far more excellent and delightful manner, and was filled with a more exceeding sweetness. She likewise gave me such an account of the sense she once had from day to day of the glory of Christ, and of God, in his various attributes, that it seemed to me she dwelt for days together in a kind of beatific vision of God, and seemed to have, as I thought, as immediate an intercourse with him, as a child with a father; and at the same time she appeared more remote from any high thought of herself, and of her own sufficiency, but was like a little child, and expressed a great desire to be instructed, telling me that she longed very often to come to me for instruction, and wanted to live at my house, that I might tell her what was her duty.[17]

The difficulty of this passage is not that its religious truth depends on a now outmoded form of discourse or that we are not told enough about the private psyche of Abigail Hutchinson to know what her life's struggle really was. The difficulty of this passage, and many others of Edwards, is that it contains the ordinary elements of daily living as they are enlarged into the illimitable perspective of God's universe. Abigail has a "sense" from "day to day" of "the glory of Christ" and of the "beatific vision of God": what the body feels, the mind knows, and what the mind knows, the soul apprehends. Abigail is unfit to trace this intricate pathway of cognition, but Edwards is not; and his narrative is the meditative recollection which the commonest words are empowered to hold and convey. The Puritan "plain style," even after it had fallen into abeyance, had been once more revived, not as the abstract phrases for Scriptural exegesis or ecclesiastical authority, but as the living of hours and days in the dark or the light which God gives men.

In the Awakening Edwards discovered history, his own and that of other men. He realized that the life-record of any person is not his alone: it is part of an enlarging continuum of God's direction for His world. What one man lives he alone has experienced, whether it were Moses, Isaiah, or Phebe Bartlet; but the narrative of one man's life becomes a paradigm for any other man who reads and heeds. The way of the light of understanding comes differently each time it is known; so too the word which conveys afterward the occasion as it was lived is understood by its own special route of apprehension: "glory," "grace," "heaven," and "hell" mean differently to men in differing times. Yet the word and the light come together in that instant configuration of the mind on its moment of knowing and ever afterward the mind is changed. Edwards knew that what he wrote and said had effects far beyond his power to measure; his words, if rightly set down, might be the instruments of conveying the light and the truth to men of later times. He could give words to experiences which men themselves did not know how to set down. The Word became for Edwards a power beyond time; in the sermon "Sinners in the Hands of an Angry God" he confronted the question of the Covenant, history (both God's and man's), and the Word in most spectacular and telling ways.

4

Because it is undoubtedly the most famous sermon ever preached on the North American continent, "Sinners in the Hands of an Angry God" has achieved a notoriety which ill accords with its purpose at the time it was delivered or its place in Edwards's thought during the most strenuous days of the

Awakening. The doctrine of the sermon rests on a theory of history already set forth in *The Work of Redemption*.

History is the record of God's fulfilling the design He had even before He created the world; and from the creation through the narratives of the patriarchs, kings, and prophets, the Old Testament is an enlarging development of all the signs and types which will be fulfilled in the birth and ministry of Christ. Single events in this great narrative, such as the captivity of the Jews into Babylon, are not dislocations or deflections of God's plan: the types of God's history all conform to the one consummation God has foreseen even before the beginning of time, and each incident in the record is a "part of one work" which forms God's cosmos. To the Puritans this great scheme of history was known as covenanted history.

When God instituted the Covenant of Grace after Adam's fall, He did so because He did not intend that all mankind should suffer and die. That many should live and sink into the anonymity of the unremembered and the lost in no wise denied God's exercise of power in behalf of those whom He had intended, even before the Fall, to redeem. Yet redemption, even for men uniquely privileged in their lifetimes to receive grace, was never assured: the elect must be those least aware that they were saved. Furthermore, the acts of grace in history were not given at once, nor were they revealed in the beginning of God's redeeming time. The Covenant was surely in effect for Abraham and his seed, even if they were unaware of it and lived too early in time to understand the profit from that divine offering. The patriarchs and prophets of the Old Testament were ministers of grace under the Covenant even before God, in the extension of His plan, fulfilled His promise by sending His Son. The times of early history were a period of slowly disappearing darkness in which the acts of grace were sure and divine but were usually unknown to the receivers of its power. In order that men in those early centuries might have some of the privileges of salvation which could come in full measure only after the Son's life, death, and resurrection, God had given to the world His "typical law"; the most important examples were, of course, the Ten Commandments; but there were other manifestations, for instance in the laws of nature and the legal systems of men. Typical law and typical history function only within those periods of time when the Covenant seems in abeyance and when men are deluded by paganism or weak in their faith; Mohammedans, worshippers of idols, and the great numbers of the unredeemed are forever in this history and law. All the while God's covenanted history goes its way and proceeds to its inevitable conclusion even when men are ignorant and there is no true church to reveal and proclaim it.

"Sinners in the Hands of an Angry God" is based on this historical-moral premise. God's Covenant of Grace, though instituted even before the world was made, can become active when men are reluctant and unwilling, for at His mere "pleasure" and by "His arbitrary will, restrained by no obligation," God may declare that covenanted history, as opposed to "typical" history, is in a new phase and must move toward the consummation He had planned for it. In reading the acrimonious debates Edwards had with his fellow divines, especially with the Reverend Charles Chauncy, the modern reader misses Edwards's insistence that the marvellous acts of grace in the 1730's and the 1740's were every moment foreordained by the terms of the Covenant God had made at Adam's fall. Divine history is covenanted history: it has its laws and movement just as does typical or mundane history; it is not a prescription to condemn the wicked and send them to writhe forever in hellfire, for they are outside the Covenant. Covenanted history and divine justice act only on the lives of those who are already in the Covenant of Grace and, most dramatically and powerfully, on those whom God intends to bring into His divine way.

Edwards's moving appeal in the sermon was that, on this very occasion in Enfield, Connecticut, and throughout the course of the Awakening, God's two laws, the typical and the moral, and His two versions of history, the mundane and the divine, had converged and were, only for this brief time, inseparable. Quite suddenly the Covenant was opened to include a wide variety of men; perhaps it would be available to all men, and then, quite as unexpectedly, the divinely propitious occasion would pass, and history might well proceed to its end with never such a time again. In "Sinners" Edwards called to three kinds of men: the wicked, who are presumably unredeemed beyond any possibility of restoration and yet who, in those transcendent moments of God's covenanted will, may be lifted at least part way to redemption; the "natural men" who love the earth and sensual things with a too great devotion but whose spirits may be rejuvenated; and lastly, the redeemed who, however, can never be sure they are saved and who, in the immeasurable trouble this world brings to men, may suffer their feet to slide in due time. To all three

Edwards addressed his ringing challenge that "Now God stands ready to pity you."

The sermon has usually been accepted as the high point of the terror Puritan ministers inflicted on their listeners, and perhaps it is. Yet the terror came not from Edwards's voice and gestures: we know that he stood fixedly in the pulpit of the Enfield church, set his eyes on the bellrope at the rear, and spoke the words in a level tone and with no high pomp of rhetoric or oratory. The feelings he aroused in his audience were not of his making; indeed, he several times admonished his listeners to stop groaning and crying aloud and to be still. True: the congregation was no doubt ready to be moved; it may even have wanted to be horrendously aroused, for writhings and contortions and shrieks were known all up and down the roads and byways where the ministers were sounding their warnings or picturing the damnation to come if men did not repent and fall on their knees.

Yet there was power and there was truth in what Edwards proclaimed in "Sinners." The truth was, and is, that man must be reborn in order to know himself as a distinctly human being and to be, in Christian terms, saved. The power lay in the effective force of language to move men beyond their common knowledge and even their normal experience. The extraordinary sermon deserves all the rhetorical and metaphorical analysis one can bring to it, for it is in its way a true work of art.

To begin, one returns to Locke's theory of language which dominated a century. If something is said from one man to another, are words real or are they only dim approximations of what was thought about in the mind of the speaker? The issue was not so much whether words represent real things or whether they cause pictures to appear in the imagination or ideas to arise in the mind; rather, it was whether words are intended and willed by the speaker or antecedently willed long before he speaks them. For Locke, words were fundamentally unreal; they were not actual, living replicas either of things they describe or of ideas in the human mind. A phrase like "the weeping stone" is an absurdity: by every evidence we have stones do not weep, and the mere whimsical joining of *stone* and *weeping* does not make anything but an impossibility. For Edwards, words, metaphors, and rhetorical devices may not be real, but they do convey real ideas located in the mind and capable of being conveyed to other minds. Time is, for example, not a thing or a substance; it is not "real"; whether it is measured as a second, an hour, or a year, it is not a sensible, knowable thing like a stone. Yet time is a very real idea by which men live and even change their world; it can be translated from one mind to another and make, as we say, sense, a something apprehended about a second, an hour, a year.

Edwards had already reasoned, and "Sinners" conforms to that reasoning, that expressions spoken or written are already willed. The very structure of language is foreordained by climate, geography, habits of people, and everything that goes to make human culture. The meanings of words necessarily require that thinking proceed from one inference to another along a route which, quite apart from any willing of the speaker, those words are destined to follow. The very logic of subject, predicate, complements, and modifiers foreordains the purpose and intention of thought; expressions of choosing, willing, desiring, and intending are, Edwards rightly saw, all antecedently predisposed by the nature of language itself. Thus words are not about real objects—the word *day* does not describe the same length of time in winter as in summer; it does not mean the same thing to a farmer as it does to a city dweller; words are, however, about real images and real ideas. Even words like *triangle, China, infinity,* and *God,* while they are not sensed and do not carry clear, specific denotations, are nevertheless capable of conducting thought from one mind to another; they are real to the extent that they move men to action, to other thought, and even to forming congeries of other ideas by which society continues to live.

Words were, for Edwards, the clearest proofs of God's Covenant with men and of God's presence in history; they have actual, sensible, "typical" meaning, and they have intelligible, moral meaning. Let us take the two in order.

Those hearers who groaned or shrieked aloud as Edwards gave his sermon were not the victims of oratorical tricks and wild mannerisms of speaking. The reason for this demonstration was that, for the "natural men" in the congregation, the words were vivid, actual carriers of God's mighty power. The images of "great waters that are dammed for the present" but which will overwhelm men once they are let loose; of the "bow of God's wrath" that "is bent" and "the arrow made ready on the string, and justice bends the bow at [the] heart, and strains the bow"; and of the "spider, or some loathsome insect, over the fire" — these were as real and powerful to those hearers as if they had been struck by a great blow or were actually on that moment feeling the intense heat of hellfire just beneath their feet.[18] For

more than a century Puritans had been so disciplined and sensi-
tized to the physical reality of words that Edwards was effectively working along lines of response to which his hearers were
well accustomed. That brilliant rhetorical trope of the spider's
dangling by a thread over a candle flame as like the perilous
state of any man's soul on this very instant was not a mere image,
a digressive embellishment of the idea of men damned or saved: it
was the living event of the human soul in the true, the actual
situation of being ultimately and eternally lost and damned.

Words convey and effect in human consciousness a true experience — an experience, indeed, more true than one may have in
daily life. But words are not made nor are they even colored by
the speaker. Edwards's impassive delivery in Enfield is indication
of how little he had to do with the rise and fall, the twist and the
involutions of his sentences. Words are (to put the idea rather
ponderously) the covenanted phenomenology of God's universe;
they were foreordained to be what they are and mean what they
mean by the initial volition of God Himself. God first had a
thought, and thus "In the beginning was the Word" — but what
word was it? It was not an actual, spoken word but rather the
covenanted genesis of all words and all languages.

Edwards's memorable sermon is, therefore, on the subject of
the will and the word. Any act that is done and every word that
is spoken are what they are because the volitional character of the
universe requires them to be so. The word — any word, every
word — is the index and key to the relation man's consciousness
has with the reality of fact and with the phenomenology of spirit.
A thought communicated, an idea given form, a concept made
manifest is not some refraction or contriving of consciousness or
mind; reality exists not as some separate entity beyond human
thinking but is itself a part and dimension of one's being. Edwards
defined the Cartesian distinction between existence and being and
Locke's line between cause and effect or substance and idea as
merely a speculative, not a radical and universal, distance. The
word is "made flesh" and becomes the real link between all things.
Yet it is not forever the same word but undergoes that actual and
speculative mutation which the varying power of God exerts.

"Sinners in the Hands of an Angry God" made the all-encompassing history of God's universe become a part of each man's
search for salvation. While the word, any word men use, is an
event in the manifestation of God's prior will in His universe, it is
nevertheless an instant wherein God acts to touch and move the

soul. By responding sensitively as they ought, men have their lives changed in the moment the two histories, the covenanted and the uncovenanted, come together. In the sermon Edwards proclaimed the wonder of the inconsistent, the provisional, and the miraculous in human life and, by showing the power of words to go beyond their common and ordinary meanings and thereby touch and penetrate the minds of men, Edwards became America's first symbolist. Language is not simply a set of figures of speech or apt metaphors in a speaker's rhetorical flight; it is a mind's renewing apprehension of its world and a fresh insight into reality. Language is, therefore, the handiwork of God in His history and another dimension of His world.

5

The World, Faith, and True Virtue

As THE first phase of the Great Awakening subsided and seemed to come to an end about 1735, Edwards felt the steady diminution of spiritual ardor among the people. He knew that numbers did not always signify the success of man's work for God; yet the painful evidence of a return to the low, insensate pleasures among the young and indifference among the old set him to wondering not only on the causes of the decline but on the actual exertions of God's will among the people. In this period between the two phases of the Awakening, extending roughly from 1735 to 1740, Edwards reviewed the work he had done and tried to answer the questions which had baffled him during the heady time of the "harvest." His thought and writing are marked in this interval by a sweet reasonableness, a gentleness and delicacy of style and spirit which the writings composed after the Awakening had flared up again and had again subsided did not match. Then Edwards was the stern logician and the angry disputant, for he had risked his whole ministry on the outcome and had presumably failed.

Three treatises mark this occasion in Edwards's thought: *Justification by Faith Alone* (1738), the *Dissertation Concerning the End for Which God Created the World*, and *The Nature of True Virtue* (the latter two published posthumouusly but produced midway in the Awakening). Their argument is quite simple — to counter and discredit the means-ends reasoning. Man does not begin life with God's bestowal of the instinct to happiness and well-being; man, by suffering and inquiry, deserves and earns understanding and joy and, perhaps, salvation. The stupefying folly of man's convincing himself that he deserves happiness and, worse, that his happiness serves the greater benefit of the world, Edwards opposed by means of the two systems of thought, Puritanism and eighteenth-century empiricism. That both were made to serve a single purpose is testimony to the nimbleness and profundity of Edwards's mind and to their cogency in one of the great arguments of the age — one in which

Berkeley, Hume, and Voltaire were, in their different guises, Edwards's partners.

We can best begin with Puritanism, with theology, for that is the starting place for Edwards's reasoning.

In *Justification by Faith Alone* — the very title is a mounting order of emphasis — Edwards declared that God's coming to and justifying man are not by virtue of man's possessing godliness as a gift of God's grace at the beginning of time: justification, or God's inclining toward man, "has no regard to anything in the person . . . as godliness, or any goodness in him"; everything that man is or has is against justification. If man, no matter how debased, still has godliness (or reason), he then merits and can even ordain his justification, for his godliness precedes and necessitates God's yielding. It "is as absurd to suppose that our godliness . . . is the ground of our justification" as it would be "to suppose that sight was prior to, and the ground of that act of mercy in Christ" when he gave sight to the man born blind. The act of mercy disposed the giving of sight — sight did not bring mercy with it. God's justification is in behalf of man's "ungodliness" — that quality and character which are against or wholly removed from God. What man is in his natural, his presumably "reasonable" being is what is most opposed to the coming of grace and his rising from the world of evil and corruption.[1]

In order that man may have salvation, two things are required. When man appears before the judgment of God, he must be pronounced just; yet his state of being justified in the world depends not on anything he has done but rather on his being delivered from the evil forces which surround and control him. Justification is one of these requirements. It was achieved by Christ's death and resurrection; but it did not bring redemption, which is to be realized only with Christ's glorious return at the end of time. Justification is already accomplished; redemption is still a question of hope for the future. Yet the assurance that Christ will return and will triumph at the end of the world is a promise that, however venal man becomes and however corrupt the world, Christ has gained the victory over the demonic forces to which man is subject.

The fact that Edwards put the emphasis for justification on "faith alone" does not mean that faith leads inevitably to the accomplishment of justification and redemption. Justification takes place in each individual life and is similarly an event in history; redemption is outside history. The teaching of some Puritan clergymen had so misconstrued the two that redemption was presumably occurring in the life of a repentant sinner the moment he sought the ways of justification; and since those ways are as many as the acts of human living, a man might convince himself of his justification simply by changing his life, doing good works, or engaging in forms of devotion and piety. Edwards put the emphasis for justification — not for redemption — on "faith alone," on that act of God's redeeming power which God alone can initiate and fulfill in the sinner. "*We are justified only by faith in Christ,*" Edwards insisted, "*and not by any manner of virtue or goodness of our own.*" Note that Edwards does not turn to an actual sin of Adam which must be rectified; he disclaims any power of "ceremonial law" or the "legal covenant," as he had formerly called it. The "law" to which God requires man to live in obedience does not bring justification; if it did, then Adam's obedience to the law after his great sin would have brought him and his children some ease from the penalty. Adam's obedience was no more a restoration of his soul than man's mere conformity to the ends for which God apparently created the world can lift and save him. And if Adam or any man, prophet or saint, had fulfilled the stipulations of God's penalty, then salvation would have been there for the asking, and justification would not have needed Christ's suffering, death, and resurrection: "Christ alone performs the condition of our justification and salvation. . . . Christ suffered the punishment of sin, not as a private person, but as our surety." [2]

Put in slightly different terms, faith is the means and justification is the end; "it was not intended," Edwards insisted, "that faith was the instrument wherewith God justifies, but the instrument wherewith we receive justification; not the instrument wherewith the justifier acts in justifying, but wherewith the receiver of justification acts in accepting justification." It "must be owned," Edwards at once admitted, that "this is an obscure way of speaking." The obscurity was not in the phrasing but in the ascription of words in common speaking to ideas which had, for the time, lost their color and currency. They might well have been understood "of old among those that then commonly used such metaphors"; they are "difficultly understood now." In words as simple as he could frame, Edwards defined "faith" and "justification": "if I should allow them to be obscure metaphors, yet so much at least is certainly plain in them, viz. that faith is that by which those who before were separated, and at a distance from Christ . . . do cease to be any longer at such a distance, and do come into that relation and nearness; unless" — and here Edwards admitted that the way was not open to everyone — "unless they are so unintelligible, that nothing at all can be understood by them." Faith is therefore "the soul's active uniting with Christ"; justification is the "action" of God from His side and at His willed determination to bring about that union.[3]

Justification is precisely like history and natural law. From the very first incentive of His will in the universe, God ordained that every act should be followed by another act and still another in the unbroken chain of His cause and effect and His means and ends. For one atom to stray or go its own way would deny God's universe; even the blind resistance of men is as rigorously part of this design as the movement of the tides and the planets. But even as He fixed the natural laws and the implacable courses of nature, God placed the principle of man's justification: God would not let man become merely another particle in a scrupulously subservient order; man must resent and rebel and then must be brought back again — not every man, to be sure, but those who would, from the beginning, be God's chosen instruments. Justification was the "legal" and the "covenanted" law and willing of God to restore man to what he had lost and to regain for him what he could not have on his own.

The direction of this reasoning is quite obvious. Edwards was countering the monstrous fallacy not only that man can save himself but that God allows man somehow to be free and by doing good works earn the right to retribution and salvation. Rather than meet this folly with the full strength of disputation, Edwards slyly insinuated the very principle of the Covenant and of history to which Puritans accorded their full acceptance but which, in every outward way, they had abandoned. To say that we gain acceptance and salvation by "merit" is not to say that we obtain it alone: if that were so, every occasion in history would be meaningless; nothing that had occurred between Adam and this present would have any relevance if God, from His side, arbitrarily selected one man for grace. History is, rather, the ever-swelling narrative of God's legal and justifying power: what happened to Adam, Abraham, Moses, and to all other men is the necessary reason for whatever happens to any man now living or yet to be born. "The adverse scheme of justification supposes that we are justified by our works," as though we can labor to deserve justification. If this were so, then our first parents and all subsequent men could have "had eternal life given them for any proper merit in their obedience," and thereby, at any time in any century, single men or whole societies, laboring diligently in the way of God, would have been lifted up and saved. The truth is quite the contrary: history and natural law have fixed the rationale of justification just as sternly as the laws of time and motion. We are justified and made one with God by that enduring Covenant of Grace whereby, through the continuity of "faith in Christ," not by single acts of our doing nor by "trusting in our own righteousness," we are brought into that full accord with that divine purpose which exists throughout all time.[4]

Edwards had most cleverly turned the means-ends argument back upon itself and reduced it to absurdity. He undercut the Arminian doctrine as cogently as anyone has by showing that God's will is God's, not man's, and that God's justifying power serves God's ends, not man's. Edwards also showed that if man's will were free to work or not work in order to gain or lose grace, then God has no means of His own, and His universe consists of no end but that which serves the capricious longings of men in some peculiar place and time. And if God sent His Son merely to palliate the distresses of men on this earth and to offer salvation for the asking, then Christ's death and resurrection were no "acquittance from our guilt" but only an interesting case of a man or god who did what man dare not and cannot do. Christ's death was a mere incident like the death of any other man, and original sin had somehow been remitted long before he was born.[5]

Edwards's insistence on justification "by faith alone" was absolute; the argument could go no other way. For man to be allowed to "merit" or to choose justification would be as senseless as his turning the laws of nature in a way different from the direction they were going. If Newton and Locke meant anything in the course of modern thought, then the rigorous, unbroken causation in the world was a reaffirmed truth — reaffirmed because the laws of motion simply buttressed the laws of God's causation. And if Locke's principle of human cognition were true (and it seemed to be), then man's very thought about faith and justification was not known only in the mind but was apprehended through all the intricate byways of sense and perceiving. Man could no more choose his becoming a child of God and an inheritor of the Kingdom of Heaven than he could determine the route of the particles of light which entered his eye or the texture of the sensation he had in the day or the night. Neither justification nor cognition is self-regulated; each is inevitable. Edwards had used the sternest and oldest doctrine of the Christian fathers and the newer system of logic to re-establish an ancient truism: man is formed not by his own will and intention but by everything that comes to him from the world of the past and of the present.

2

Edwards's most noteworthy answer to Arminianism was *The Nature of True Virtue*, that least polemical and most sweetly reasoned of all his writings. Quite obviously its reasoning was gentle, for it was treating that gentle, reasonable theme "virtue." It comes not long after *Justification by Faith Alone* and is a companion to the *Dissertation Concerning the End for Which God Created the World*. The very titles are suggestive with their key words "Faith," "Virtue," and "End." They come from the very center of the eighteenth-century principle concerning man's place and the means and ends of life. Another curiosity of *The Nature of True Virtue* is that its argument was conducted almost wholly without Scriptural authority. Biblical names are referred to only as passing illustrations, much as secular precedents are cited. So to reduce Scriptural authority is not to suggest that Holy Writ does not sustain true virtue; it is rather to suppose that the logic of virtue is self-enclosed and that to introduce Scriptural proofs would be no more germane than to offer scientific or economic proofs. Or, perhaps, all these "proofs" are germane, for virtue is the whole of life and living.

The Nature of True Virtue is a treatise in definition of "the good." It is not concerned with daily, worldly value; it is an analysis of virtue from the highest ethical point of view — that of God Himself. By reason of its concern with divine scrutiny and judgment, it omits those argumentative bases for judging virtue and vice which Edwards's age, like any other, finds comfortable and appropriate. Yet, if the treatise looks at virtue from the absolute and divine point of view, it does not rest only on heavenly surmises: it seeks to detail the good and the beautiful in human life because each hour and day of living are parts of a divine program. Man becomes good because God, in the act of justifying grace, bestows goodness on him; and his life becomes joyous and beautiful because the divine will makes all living shine with the radiance of God's power. Man does not earn or gain virtue; rather, "true virtue" comes as a divine end to the means of justification and grace.

Edwards first made virtue consist in its agreement "to Being in general." [6] "Being" and "in general" are old and favorite terms with Edwards: the first is that existence and eternity of God which God, by His prior willing, has consented to share with men; it is thus "in general" because it is an emanation co-eternal with God and yet given the power to assume earthly and mortal form. Mankind has that much of "Being in general" as God has given them in His two major manifestations — the physical-phenomenal world and the antecedent will and choice in the election of certain of the children of men. The phrase can never be construed as "existence in particular," for it is ineffable, indefinable, and irreducible to the gross, misleading language of men.[7]

His "Being in general" is not God's bewildering abstraction; Edwards, like Augustine, Cudworth, and the Cambridge Platonists, conceived that God's emanation was "beauty," the inconceivable, all-embracing co-existence between God and His universe. This beauty is twofold. "Particular" beauty is "that by which a thing appears beautiful when considered only with regard to its connexion with, and tendency to some particular things within a limited, and as it were, a private sphere." Here is the prudential organization of means and ends wherein daily acts accord with self-love and self-ends; they are not wrong, but simply provisional and temporary. "General" beauty is, in Edwards's clear definition, "that by which a thing appears beautiful when viewed most perfectly, comprehensively and universally, with regard to all its tendencies, and its connexions with every thing it stands related to." Edwards employed an illustrative example: just as "a few notes in a tune" may sound harmonious when considered with all the notes of the tune, they may be harsh and discordant with respect to "the entire series of sounds." General beauty is "true virtue" and is "related to every thing that it stands in connexion with"; it "consists in benevolence to Being in general," or, "to speak more accurately, it is that consent, propensity and union of heart to Being in general, that is immediately exercised in a general good will."

Edwards's definition is not so much difficult as it is deficient in those clarifying opposites of term and logic by which definitions stand. Beauty "in general" is not Platonic beauty — a something-other perceived when one's perceptions have ascended from the low to the exalted along the ladder of intellect and spirit; it is not that which is agreed upon by men in a time as a "general" beauty, for such beauty and virtue would be a mere transience; nor is it esthetic beauty, the "beautiful" which, as in Shaftesbury's ethic, exists even beyond men's perceptions and animates them to be and do even beyond their knowing. Edwards means beauty and virtue "absolutely considered" as a "benevolence" toward and a pure love of God. Daily acts of love are particulars of this beauty, but the beauty of the kind he is defining transcends self-love or love of another and comes to yearn for the unattainable, in "this absolute benevolence." [8]

Even though private and public morality accords with the absolute virtue and beauty, the mere doing of good deeds need not be virtuous and laudable. Private affection, exercising itself in small, limited ways, clashes with other private interests; affections overlap, for children, friends, country: can all these, Edwards asked, be accorded the same degree of praise or blame? If they vary in value, then they are not "virtue"; true virtue does not stand in the way of favor or disfavor. Furthermore, private affections or self-love allows for its opposite, for disaffection and for enmity; love is negated by hate, and the "consent" which should arise from one's self to "Being in general" is lost or dissipated. Finally, private self-love sets up a graded authority, a cash value for virtue which, if the world pays well in its coin, God does not warrant. The conclusion is that "the true goodness of a thing . . . must be its agreeableness to its *end*, or its fitness to answer the design for which it was made"; the "inanimate and unintelligent world being made for the rational and moral" ends just as "a house is prepared for the inhabitants," the ultimate value of beauty and virtue is in accord with "the last end for which God has made all things." [9] The true test for virtue is its absolute value in the mind of God alone.

It was in what he called "secondary" or the commonly understood meaning of beauty or virtue — that "which consists in a mutual consent and agreement of different things in form . . . called by the various names of regularity, order, uniformity, symmetry, proportion, [and] harmony" — that Edwards made his most complete assault, albeit a sweetly reasonable and guileless one, on the doctrine of means and ends. This "secondary" beauty can be seen and appreciated in the "mutual agreement" of the three sides of a triangle, in the parts of a regular polygon, in the colors of "chintz or brocade," and in "the beautiful proportion of the various parts of an human body." [10] Edwards rightly cited Francis Hutcheson as the leading spokesman for this view which allows things to have beauty as they are considered in themselves as "beautiful" and yet conceives of their beauty as sharing in that grand design which leads ultimately to a "cordial" and natural symmetry and agreement throughout the universe.[11]

Edwards arrayed his points in argument carefully, for this reasoning on beauty and virtue was the main assumption of the age. It granted autonomy to the whole, the while it allowed nimble speculations on the immediate and the particular: the mind could ascend to the top of the universal order and then return at ease to the mundane and trivial, for everything was bound in a harmony which was everywhere and equally apparent. Edwards countered the well-known sensationalist moral system by showing that observations on the symmetry of the world are in no wise the "perception of the same thing which *God* is pleased to have regard to, as the ground or rule by which he has established such a law of nature." The knowing of a law of nature is not the same as the perception of the idea of God. This prudential and secondary form of beauty is often confused with size: the grander the object the greater its value and admiration. Furthermore, this apparent symmetry or dissimilarity is subject to endless partitioning: the whole building can be particled into its cornices, panels, and pilasters; a musical composition is capable of reduction to its single notes; even if the whole structure is reconstituted, it remains in its beauty tenuously riven between the exquisite elements and the full design. Lastly, in this argument, Edwards showed that a theory of beauty as symmetry confuses physical and spiritual forms; the something called "beautiful" is not to be construed with the "beauty in the virtue called *justice*"; and to reason from the symmetry of the thing to the beauty of the ideal is utterly to confuse physical sensations with abstract perception. The ideal is beautiful to the degree that it conforms to its own principle, its ideality; and the thing is graceful and symmetrical to the extent of its according with what it is or is supposed to be. Things and ideas may be both beautiful, but they are not beautiful and virtuous to the same degree or in the same way. Edwards showed that the argument becomes circular: for such a theorist as William Wollaston, God's love and being are manifested in beautiful forms which give rise to beautiful ideals and moral principles which are, in turn, the only ways of apprehending the God who designed them.[12]

Having considered the moral-sense logic of beauty — the idea that the human mind moves through degrees of beauty to the apprehension of the Beautiful — Edwards then turned to another common argument of his age, namely, the principle of self-love, which he defined, in a most rudimentary phrase, as "a man's love of his own happiness." The notion, he knew, was "absurd": "that a man, in general, loves and is pleased with happiness, or . . . has a capacity for enjoying happiness, cannot be the reason why such and such things become his happiness." Is the good one's neighbor does a "good" because it brings pleasure to the receiver or because it conforms to what the receiver already has in mind as being the proper behavior of neighborliness? The absurdity of the "notion" of self-love is that "the effect is made the cause of that, of which it is the effect: Our happiness, consisting in the happiness of the person beloved, is made the cause of our love to that person. Whereas, the truth plainly is, that our love to the person is the cause of our delighting, or being happy in his happiness." [13] Though self-love may be a "private interest" and concern only one's private being, it is never a flexible mode of inclining or choice, for it necessarily conforms to a graded scale of values. We love some things more than we love others; we avoid some matters and we seek others; we are therefore already predisposed to feel about things in the precise way we do feel about them.

Edwards showed the other fallacy in the theory of self-love. Supposedly, self-love is a kind of neutral ground whereon, at any moment, a choice can be made between rejection and acceptance, between what displeases and what pleases. The fact is, as Edwards insisted, that to have or be in the state of self-love one must earlier have been in and passed through what was not self-love. To know pleasure one must have known pain; to know love one must already have felt hate. Thus emotion and feeling are those infinitely variable distances between opposites; and self-love is never neutral and self-regulated but ever predisposed by the necessities which make men feel at all. (Edwards would most cogently return to this argument in his *Freedom of the Will*.)

In order fully to discredit the moral theory of self-love, Edwards considered the behavior of one who is presumably acting in accordance with its premise. When one considers his choices in selecting what he likes and what he dislikes, he tends to break down the acts of choosing into smaller and smaller segments of choice. A man says he "likes" or approves of justice; it enhances and makes life tolerable; so a just law benefits one's town and county; so too the actions of a just man radiate throughout a community and thereby form units of single acts of self-love for and among one's fellows. The fallacy in such reasoning is, not that one has moved from the general idea of justice to the specific act of doing a just thing, but that, in the very act of moving along a scale, one has been predisposed to make just those distinctions along the way of graded authority in just the way they were made. If self-love is never "free" — and it is never free — then it cannot be considered a virtue. It is simply a form of instinct and common behavior.

Edwards was not content with undermining such commonplace moral ideas as the principle of moral beauty and self-love; he considered that new and fashionable scheme of the eighteenth century which, dignified by the teachings of moral system-makers like Shaftesbury and the Scottish moralists and popularized by a fashionable moral intellectualism of the day, went by the name of moral-sense philosophy. After Edwards's death it would virtually usurp moral philosophy in American schools and colleges; when Hawthorne was at Bowdoin, and Emerson at Harvard, and while Melville was pondering in his own way the issues of fate and foreknowledge, this system had gained all the authority of virtually universal acclaim. It took a revolution in moral thinking to overturn it; Utilitarianism, a variation on self-love, accomplished that feat.

Moral-sense logic is itself a version of the principle of self-love. It supposes that, above the petty demands of one's willing and nilling, of desiring and repelling, of accepting and rejecting, is a human authority which does not accord with one's single purposes. Men make sacrifices of their wages and even of themselves in order that some grand aim higher than their selfish desires may be accomplished. To be sure, that higher aim may accord with their selfishness: the improvement of one's community eventually enhances one's own life. Nonetheless, in the history of mankind signal acts of devotion have been so frequent as to grant to many men the accolade that they acted on principles of sacrifice and conduct higher than self-satisfaction; they were moved by the "moral sense."

Edwards's approach to this principle was precise and devastating. Suppose, he asked, that all men who seek virtue do have a moral sense: do they all have it to the same amount and in the same degree? If they have, then we can substitute "ourselves in their stead." But no man can put himself in another's place: if he does, he is no longer "himself" but has made "such an alteration, as to degree and circumstances," of "shape, size, complexion, situ-

ation, and motion of their bodies" that he has denied his own
moral sense for the sake of achieving another. The substitution of
oneself for another is an impossibility: we are ever ourselves; our
experience is ours only. "We never could have any notion what
understanding or volition, love or hatred are, either in created
spirits or in God, if we had never experienced what understanding and volition, love and hatred, are in our minds." Knowing
only ourselves, we merely transfer or ascribe to others what we
already feel and believe.[14]

Suppose, however, that we were able to put ourselves in others'
places: we make their pains and pleasures ours. In so doing we
have at once denied the principle of self-love and abrogated our
own moral sense. Yet, even so, this abrogation may lead to the
Christian ideal of charity and a "natural conscience," as Edwards
called it, which fulfills the demand that a man lose himself in
order that he may find himself. If this principle of moral sense
and of self-loss were an accurate description of the way toward
love of God, then it would still be inadequate: it would require
that we make ourselves, our wills, and our beings subserve now
one and now another of our fellows. We would be ever the prey
of demands made on us by our contemporaries and thereby we
would never seek the ideal of virtue in God. The moral-sense
logic may very well make us conform to the ways of the world; it
would become, for Franklin, a marvellous key to proper social
and political behavior, but it would never create what Edwards
and Emerson knew was the true and proper end of a man,
namely, Character, which rests not on approbation or condemna-
tion, not on inward self-esteem, and certainly not on self-satisfaction.

Then what is "true virtue"? Even though Edwards spent more
time defining what it is not than what it might be, he nonetheless
in the final chapter of his treatise reached a conclusion of his
argument: "virtue is a certain kind of beautiful nature, form, or
quality that is observed in things. That form or quality is called
beautiful," he went on, "which appears in itself agreeable or
comely, . . . or the view or idea of which is immediately pleasant to the mind." So far Edwards has not gone beyond principles
such as self-love or "natural agreeableness." However, he went
on: "I say agreeable *in itself*, and *immediately* pleasant, to distin-
guish it from things which in themselves are not agreeable nor
pleasant, but either indifferent or disagreeable. . . . But when a
form or quality appears lovely, pleasing and delightful in itself,

then it is called beautiful; and this agreeableness or gratefulness of the idea is what is called beauty." But how, one may ask, does one achieve this idea of beauty?

The answer is that we accomplish it in two ways. One way is that we build it around and outside ourselves; we find it by means of locating ourselves amid those infinite numbers of things which agree and those which disagree, those which instantly attract and those which all our lives repel us. This ordering of parts or a "consent of things to other things" is a moral workmanship which has already been given us. We therefore build this "consent" because we must, for we live not in units and particles but with everything that conforms to a master principle existing in the world long before we came into it. Thus "beauty" is the appreciation of a stern and symmetrical moral order evident, even as are laws of nature, throughout God's universe.

The second way we know beauty is little more than an intellectual and moral deepening of the first. Whatever we apprehend as beauty or truth is, even as we are realizing it, in precise agreement with the divine Beauty we are in the process of knowing. Yet what the mind comes to know is not an activity or a process: we do not quicken or enlarge our perceptions as we can make our hands more skillful at their craft. The "immediate presence of the beautiful idea depends," Edwards reasoned, "not, therefore, on any reasonings about the idea, after we have it," but "on the frame of our minds." The "frame of our minds" was what was given us at our birth; thus it is not wholly our own but, having been held in trust for us as part of our legacy as children of God, is bestowed upon us and made one of the talents with which we are entrusted.

Beauty and virtue are ours — and they are not ours. They belong to us because we make them a part of our being and we give them something of our own character. But they are not ours, because to have them is to be aware of their antecedence to the beginning of time. Virtue is, accordingly, a form of history, for, in whatever way we are aware of it, it "is agreeable to the necessary nature of things" and to that unchanging "true virtue" which exists only in the mind of God.[15] Man does not have beauty; he does not possess character: he has beauty and character bestowed on him by means of his inheritance as a child of God. Beauty is the mark God set on every act and thought; afterward He allows man to understand it.

The argument is for moral necessitarianism: man is most moral when he is doing what he must do; an immoral or an ugly act is inconceivable because the universe prevents the slightest infraction or variance. Yet, in *The Nature of True Virtue*, Edwards was not content to refute the fashionable systems of moral theory: at the conclusion of the treatise he resorted to the idea of language left over from Locke's *Essay Concerning Human Understanding*. Although he would later raise the same issue in the *Freedom of the Will*, he employed it with considerable deftness in *The Nature of True Virtue*.

The languages of men contain "terms . . . by which things of a moral nature are signified" and "express those moral sentiments or ideas which are common to mankind." Those words which connote "right and wrong, good and evil," signify those things which "deserve praise or blame, respect or resentment." Men who speak those words of good and evil, praise and blame, do not on the instant invent those words nor are those words determined to have just those meanings "by the nature of things" but, rather, "by the sentiments of men with relation to the nature of things." The meanings of words are, therefore, not casual or accidental but "extremely various" according to the custom, the geography, and the history of a people who use them. Words in common, daily use are for daily purposes; they are the modes of action in sustaining life; and they may pass out of common currency with the changing behavior of men. Yet even the differing words and the varieties of meanings of good or evil, praise or blame, do have "uniformity."

The troublesome inconsistencies of words and the striking diversity of dialects in the world do not deny that "uniformity" which the world's languages possess. "Mankind in general" does maintain "some general standard or foundation in nature for an universal consistence in the use of the terms whereby they express moral good and evil." Thus language is both the transitory reflection of habits and moral ideas which men have in a place and time and also a total, coherent system of logic and meaning which God has intended and which languages maintain throughout all time.[16]

By showing that words are themselves regulated and already predispose the moral meanings they convey — the word "desire" moves toward some culmination of wish or longing; the word "good" inherently contains those meanings that the four letters foreordain — Edwards had overcome the chief objections of the means-and-ends argument, the theory of self-love, and the principle of moral sense. If the very words "means and ends," "self-love," and "moral sense" are logical structures having life and duration in human thought beyond the fashions of a time, then language is like nature, a route of cognitive activity: it exists both in the minds of men and even outside human consciousness when thought is inert and the mind is asleep. Words predispose every thought man will have, for they, like God's own will and the laws of nature, are aspects of that continuum of consciousness into which men are born and in which for a time they live. Man does not make the laws of nature; he hardly varies the implication of a word he uses, and he surely is not free to shift the burden of moral understanding by so much as a mathematical fraction. Language, that commonest thing human thought uses, suggests that man is but a minute part of an infinite perspective. What he learns he must know, and what he discovers as the truth of moral virtue was ever there for his comprehension. "Virtue" is living and thinking in concert with the infinitude of God's universe.

3

The Nature of True Virtue defined a human morality. Its companion piece, the *Dissertation Concerning the End for Which God Created the World*, considered the nature of virtue from God's side. The central question raised by the *Dissertation* might be interpreted as that posed by a universe flawed from the start: God's "end" in creation was surely thwarted by the very means He employed; man fell and brought sin and death into the world. Or the question might be construed as one more inquiry into the nature of original sin. The "end" for which God created the world could hardly have been for the reason that He might witness the corruption of His handiwork and watch the painful lives of His helpless creatures. Modern commentators relish such a view, for it exonerates God by giving Him the role of supreme tragedian in a tragic universe. Original sin becomes, therefore, the one bond between debased man and tragic God; each in some way appreciates the sensitivity of the other.

On the issue of a flawed universe, Spinoza had identified evil with defect of knowledge or with non-being. Evil is mere appearance; our conception of it is possible only if we can look at things *sub specie aeternitatis*. Indeed, an inquiry into the problem of the origin of sin, whether original or not, is superfluous. Leibniz had distinguished "moral" evil from "metaphysical" evil by reason of the necessary imperfection of all things finite. He seemed to re-

gard all souls as existing in the inevitable aftermath of Adam's fall;
and since human nature is flawed by that imperfection of man's
beginning, then the question of the "end" for which God created
the world is implicit in the beginning: man was created in imperfection and all his history is but a paraphrase of that primary law.

Edwards's *Dissertation Concerning the End for Which God
Created the World* supposed, first, that God created the world to
suit His own purposes, the chief of which was "His glory"; sec-
ondly, that the universe of His creation serves purposes beyond
man's existence, even if it seems to serve his benefit and joy; and
thirdly, that excellence and virtue are part of a universe of value:
if anything is rightly valuable at one point, it is valuable and
virtuous at all other points. The *Dissertation* is one answer to the
riddle of original sin; it begins with the common means-ends assumptions of the time and then transcends them by one of Edwards's most cogent arguments.

The atom may display as much "true virtue" as a star; and, if
read aright, the ant speaks truth as clearly as does a man. If one
argues that the world is the handiwork of the Deity and displays
everywhere His beneficent hand, then all one need do is to worship the grand laws of nature and be virtuous: the worm and the
moldwarp are exemplars and texts. Or, if one sees the physical
world as a projection of man and his intelligence, then anything
in reality is but the breath and muscle of humanity caught just
short of its universal display: a face looms in the cloud bank, a
color like the color of the eye is held in the water, and man need
but glance and everything reflects himself and his soul. Edwards
was too stern and logical ever to sink into these amiable fallacies.

In order to settle the means-ends argument, the slippery principle of self-love, and the questionable illusion of man's moral
sense, Edwards had to trace virtue and even all thought back to
God's first intention and idea. To be sure, God did not have a
"first" intention: to have had an intention in the beginning would
suggest that it was subject to variation and that God could act
counter to it in the course of universal history. Thus as a way of
avoiding the ambiguity of ascribing to God an intention which
could be modified, Edwards used the word "end"; God had
"ends" which were coordinate with His being: ". . . *a disposition in God, as an original property of his nature, to an emanation
of his own infinite fulness, was when excited him to create the
world; and so that the emanation itself was aimed at by him as a
last end of the creation.*" [17]

Yet not all ends served precisely the one divine "end": the manner of God's working was proper to the end He had in mind and consistent with the way He would reveal Himself to the children of men. Even if man mistook what God had intended — the history of the Old Testament Jews seemed a tragic record of such misunderstanding — the apparent failure of one end but served the grander, final end God had in view when He created the world. The end for which the Jews had been chosen prepared for the coming of the Son; the end which He died in order to serve was misconstrued by the apostles and the early church; yet that divine end did not fail, for it prepared for the resurgence of belief and hope in the latter hours of God's time. Thus God's supreme end was beyond man's comprehension; this Edwards called an "ultimate end," one which could never be completed even in the last hour of universal time: it was the "end" for which God had created the world. "In fine," Edwards wrote, "God, being, as it were, an all comprehending Being, all his moral perfections, as his holiness, justice, grace and benevolence are some way or other to be resolved into a supreme and infinite regard to himself; and if so it will be easy to suppose that it becomes him to make himself his supreme and last end in his works." [18]

If this ultimate end were all that God had ever conceived, then He would forever be unknown; and if His wisdom and prescience were sufficient only to Him and proved only by His majesty, then men would have no more virtue than the insects and beasts. It was the something-other which God, by a reduction or lessening of His will, had given to man and revealed in the world which had permitted man to be a child of God and a being created in His image. By diminishing His godhood, by being provisionally less than God, God could be known by man and man be wise. Thus Edwards conceived of "subordinate ends" which are God's permissive demonstrations of what is less than Himself in order that men may know Him. These lesser ends cannot go counter to the ultimate end; all the subordinate ends together are of less worth than the one grand end. Edwards reasoned that "the subordinate effects, events, or things brought to pass, which are all means of this end, all [unite] to contribute their share towards the obtaining the one last end." [19]

At once the argument becomes facile and slippery. If God has an ultimate end which all the various subordinate ends serve, then man should be able to inquire into these secondary ends and, by relating them in some logical order, deduce the ultimate end God

had in mind. The reasoning verged perilously on that favorite
Puritan rationale of "second cause" which is the lower, mundane
disclosure of the absolute intention; and if Edwards conformed to
that argument, he need only write a study of the human mind
creating God in its own image. Edwards considered instead the
very difficult question of being and non-being, entity and nonentity.

Suppose that God had an intention or end which was coterminous with His being: that intention would be, of course, timeless
and limitless; it would, furthermore, partake of God's pure being
because it co-existed with Him; it would be "being" in its purest
form. Similarly, all that was not of the being of God did not have
existence and could not thereby manifest His end and intention.
To posit such a principle would be, however, an impossibility:
non-being and nonentity are not the opposite or the absence of
God. They are what are left behind and are out of consideration
when God is not thinking of them: for God not to be thinking of
them and not to have them as part of His intention is to make
them inconceivable; they do not have the first principle of His
intention; they are not of or from His being and knowing.

Thus being and non-being, entity and nonentity, are not opposites in God's universe: for to affirm that God has "being" is to
define the total being of His universe. Non-being is what Edwards called the "defect" or God's willing suspension of His
godhead for the sake of having an end and giving existence to
creation. "It is a thing infinitely good in itself," Edwards wrote in
the *Dissertation*, "that God's glory should be known by a glorious
society of created beings. . . . If existence is more worthy than
defect and nonentity, and if any created existence is in itself worthy to be, then knowledge or understanding is a thing worthy to
be." [20] Knowledge is the manifestation of God's being displayed
along the route of those subordinate ends which all together co-
exist with and lead to that ultimate end for which the universe
was created.

It is well enough to say, as Edwards was saying, that God
created the world to give being to that which would otherwise
have to endure non-being; and if God so conceived His act of
creation, then He presumably bestowed "pleasure" on that portion of existence by removing it from "nonentity and defect."
The argument again verged on the pleasure-pain principle: what
had given God pleasure to conceive and create thereby forever
contained His emanation of pleasure, and man had but to know it

and derive pleasure from it. Edwards stalwartly resisted any suggestion that God's antecedent pleasure was the means for giving the world or mankind something that would be or become pleasant. What moved God to create the world and thereby to bestow being on His creatures was "a glorious and abundant emanation of His infinite fulness of good *ad extra*, or without himself." That "disposition to communicate himself, or diffuse his own FULNES," as an emanation of His pure being, was what created the world. He conceived it, first, as an extension of His being: creation is that much of God in His "fulnes" which is not a spiritual emanation but which is the embodied form of His delight. But His delight is not in what He has created: if it were, then that joy has suffered grievous diminution in the course of centuries.[21] Rather, His delight and the ultimate end of all His works are summarized "in that one phrase, *the glory of God;* which is the name by which" God knows Himself and His own being throughout all time and by which "the last end of God's works is most commonly called." Both means and ends are served in the being of God; and all effects are but "emanations of God's glory." "Now God's glory," Edwards continued, is both a self-sufficient joy of God in His own being and an "emanation or communication" of that "internal glory or fulness of God as it is." His beneficence, His knowledge and will, exist before any creature exists; and He created life, not because He enjoys the subordination of lives in dependence upon Him, but because His emanation is its own joy and end; they begin and are simultaneously fulfilled in "his holiness and happiness." [22]

By willing less than His godhead, God revealed His good and glory in "these three things, viz. his infinite knowledge; his infinite virtue or holiness, and his infinite joy and happiness." These are, properly speaking, "attributes in God"; but they remained not His attributes alone; they were shared with men. His knowledge became, however dimly, man's knowledge, not as a direct revelation but as a continued "emanation" of the being and fullness of God in all its power and radiated might. His "infinite virtue or holiness" was partially bestowed on man by reason of God's communicating "the love of himself"; thus man's knowing God becomes a love of God in all His supreme virtue; thereafter, man loves his fellow man and even himself. God's "infinite joy and happiness" are revealed to men who know God's "excellency," love God for it, and rejoice in it. Thus, though the glory and knowledge of God consist of a wholly "internal glory," for

He alone possesses and knows them, they are a "refulgence" or an "emanation" which shines upon man "and is reflected back to the luminary. The beams of glory come from God, and are something of God, and are refunded back again to their original. So that the whole is *of* God, and *in* God, and *to* God, and God is the beginning, middle and end." [23]

God did not, therefore, bestow good on man or place a principle of joy and goodness in His universe. Goodness and happiness come not from man's deserving but from his making his union with God "his ultimate end." "When the happiness is perfect, the union is perfect." To be sure, there never will be a time "when it can be said, the union is now infinitely perfect": God's justice can never be satisfied, even with the damnation of the last sinner or the elevation of the final saint. The end is in the beginning, and the beginning foreordained the end. "It is certain," Edwards wrote near the end of the *Dissertation Concerning the End for Which God Created the World,* "that what God aimed at in the creation of the world, was the good that would be the consequence of the creation, in the whole continuance of the thing created." This reasoning might not satisfy the "modern free thinkers, who do not like the talk about satisfying justice with an infinite punishment," for, as Edwards well knew, it put the emphasis of the cosmos rightly where it belonged — on God the creator and not on man the receiver.[24]

4

Once again Edwards had put a counterweight on a segment of eighteenth-century thought, first by showing the ambiguities and fallacies which inhered in the very thought itself and then by posing a principle loftier than a mere mechanism. For what was wrong with moral-sense logic of the eighteenth century was not a confusion between means and ends or the ascription of a principle of morality to man when it denied any morality in the world: for man to possess self-love meant that he alone had it by a single, unique act of God's bestowal. The fault in these nimbly posed moral theories was that they denied any intimate relation between man and God and thus, all the while they granted man the privilege of standing solidly in his world, they left him as bereft as Crusoe on his forlorn island. The eighteenth century never lived to see this peril, but two later centuries did: when man makes himself the measure of his own moral scheme, he abandons himself to the peril of his own consciousness which, without support of anything but itself, construes a world in its own image and finally comes to rest in the interior darkness of each man's private terror. The other flaw in eighteenth-century moral theory was that it lacked, quite simply, a heart. It would exalt "the man of feeling," the Rousseauistic sentimentalist who bled at the slightest hurt to nature and to living things, and the passionate libertarian who might even risk death for the sake of a cause. It still lacked a heart; and when the Romantic conscious-ness discovered that emptiness, it filled the lack with the intensest recoil of the private self known to history. It fashioned "the Romantic revolution," not as a protest against evil and the world, but as a desperate necessity for each living heart to discover itself, not as the world saw it, but as the soul and mind alone can envi-sion. The Romantic journey of consciousness, from Goethe, Wordsworth, Poe, to Verlaine and Proust became the latter-day counterpart to that inquiry into the mysterious self which Ed-wards had conducted.

For one of the last occasions when such a union was possible, Edwards had joined a Puritan ethic with an empiricist's demand that the cause of moral thinking be construed according to the way most men lived their lives. The result was a form of extrem-ism, a moral baroque as colorful and gorgeously designed as a mural by Tintoretto. The outcome was a moral inscrutabil-ity: God could not be seen because He was illimitable; yet He had revealed His purposes for men in eternal forms which were there for men's apprehension. Owing to the fatal and pervasive flaw which ever darkens man's vision — the very condition of his being a human being — man could see and know these principles only by the most arduous struggles and the intensest concentra-tion of his powers. Nothing less than divine perfectibility was the demand; and nothing more than the painful accord with the world as it is was the human possibility. Even as his contemporar-ies set the moral law lower and lower and made ethical thinking conform ever more readily to commerce and daily rectitude, Ed-wards raised the necessity higher.

Yet, whereas the century made the world the measure of man, Edwards finally made man his own measure — not that "man" which comes as our credit with the rest of the race, but that highest being of ourselves which we can know only when we live at the very top of our spiritual intensity. The moral life could be, therefore, the equivalent of a work of art.

6

Sovereign God and Humbled Man

EDWARDS'S own ministry after 1740 moved toward ever-increasing power over men in the Connecticut Valley until the second phase of the Awakening waned and finally came to an end sometime in 1742. That was to be all; Edwards would never again have a "harvest of souls." Indeed, his preaching, while it had brought hundreds to the knowledge of the Lord, had got him into trouble in his own church in Northampton. He had more and more insistently required that those who in his parish and under his special guidance professed themselves to be true Christians and desired to enter the church should be inquired into for the depth of their conversion and their new faith. The very requirement seemed to many like a return to a way of life as fallacious as a belief in witchcraft; Edwards's own grandfather, the sainted Solomon Stoddard, had long held that no man was empowered to look into the human heart and judge whether it were saved. "My honoured grandfather Stoddard," Edwards wrote in a letter, "strenuously maintained the Lord's Supper to be a *converting ordinance;* and urged all to come, who were not of a scandalous life, though they knew themselves to be unconverted. I formerly conformed to his practice; but I have had difficulties with respect to it, which have been long increasing; till I dared no longer proceed in the former way; which has occasioned great uneasiness among my people, and has filled all the country with noise. . . ." [1] Edwards demanded that the confessed sinner who wished to be accepted in the church and to receive the Lord's Supper should submit himself to those tests of faith by the minister and the ruling elders which had fallen into abeyance.

Yet, during the high emotion of the Awakening, the number of confessed sinners was so great that the administration of an inquiry into men's states of mind and soul was little more than a formality. Quite obviously God was working with remarkable effect, and the official sanction of the ministers and the elders was hardly necessary to receive the confessed sinner into the flock: one day's, one hour's loss might mean the difference between eternal life and eternal death in the world to come; and what minister or elder would dare pronounce the verdict on the depth of conversion in the presence of such awful responsibility? Yet, as the weeks and months passed and the Holy Spirit seemed not to inflame the people as it had formerly done, those few who came to the front of the church and pled to be admitted into the company of the faithful seemed to be men and women of lesser conviction and weaker power than those who had asked for admission in the days of emergent occasions. Some of these suppliants were, on only cursory examination, found grievously wanting in fervor and dedication. More significantly, with the waning of the Awakening, Edwards watched with dismay the people of Northampton and its environs — the very ones who just a few months before had professed their absolute reliance on God's calling and His mercies — abandoning their spiritual exercises and returning to the taverns, gamings, and "frolics in the night." Edwards was coming to realize that outward professions of a new life and the public acknowledgment of God as master and Jesus as redeemer were not clear signs of a truly changed spirit: hypocrites and sinners had come into the company of Zion, and now they were falling away; so too those of a vague and tenuous hold on the truths of God, even though they might for a time have been brought a little closer than they had been to the recognition of God and His Son, had not been truly redeemed. Whose fault was it that the new harvests had failed and that people were as recalcitrant as they had ever been before the enlivenings of conscience?

Edwards displayed, after 1742, that characteristic of his mind which has not endeared him to readers of a later time unused to the profound disappointment a man can feel when he has failed from reasons quite out of his making and control. It was not his fault, it was certainly not God's fault, that the loss of zeal was apparent in the land. The Word had been spoken: it was God's, not the minister's, Word, and the ears that had opened were now closed again. As the months passed into 1743 Edwards's prose became dark with warnings and his scorn was almost apocalyptic. "How did this practice come in with you in particular?" he asked in his sermon entitled "Joseph's Great Temptation and Gracious Deliverance," the practice of flouting the words of the Lord, "You that two or three years ago, seemed to be so engaged in religion? Did it not come in, did you not begin to practise it, as the sense of religion wore off? And what is the matter? Why did not you set up the practice then, when your heart was taken up about reading, meditation, and secret prayer to God? If this do not at all stand in the way of them, and is no hindrance to them, why was you not engaged in both together? What account can you give of it?" Edwards ended by abandoning the elder people to their just condition and yet warned them to look to their children, since "Satan doubtless would be glad to have such an interest amongst us as he used to have." [2]

2

The Edwards who preached the sermons of the Awakening was also the Edwards who continued to follow the intellectual and meditative habits of a lifetime. The sermons have assumed, in the two centuries since they were delivered, the coloring of terror and the vividness of hellfire; they were not so in their own time: they were clearly reasoned analyses of the varieties of a man's religious experience — his daily, living experience — in concert with his Maker. Indeed, as the harvest of souls declined, Edwards turned more and more, not to seeking out those proofs of the abundance of God's work with His people not to the accomplishment which had, despite the sudden decline, been evident in the community and throughout the surrounding countryside, but to the instants and particulars of religious feeling which would become, for him who received it aright, religious thought. In the waning of the Awakening which seemed to prove what its enemies had charged, namely, that religious emotion had little or nothing to do with religious conversion and salvation, Edwards set out in the middle forties to announce triumphantly the truth of personal emotion and the consequence in the accession of God's light of most private feeling.

Boldly Edwards sought to explore those moments which had occurred in the lives of Abigail Hutchinson and Phebe Bartlet but which can come to any man whom God has elected or who is aroused in his heart to learn the deep things God wants him to know. What had just happened in New England was, Edwards learned, happening with remarkable similarity in Scotland. Indeed, the Scottish clergy sent over an invitation that the brethren of the churches separated by the Atlantic Ocean should join in "an union of prayer" on appointed Tuesdays, Thursdays, and Saturdays. Edwards published a memorial eloquently supporting this cause which might unite men and advance God's kingdom on earth.[3] He was aided in this cause by an association with a remarkable young man, the Reverend David Brainerd, a minister of

great promise who was by 1747 engaged to Edwards's beloved daughter Jerusha. Edwards had heard of Brainerd even
before their association: in 1743 Brainerd had been dismissed
from Yale for casually remarking of one of his teachers, "He
has no more grace than this chair." After his dismissal Brainerd
had become dedicated to unpopular causes, especially to the
cause of revivals; and with the seeming failure of the Awakening, Edwards was attracted to this vivacious young man whose
whole life and ministry were bent on touching men's souls and
who had so little respect for the successful ways some clergymen followed that he was happy in his work as missionary
to the Christian Indians in New Jersey. But David Brainerd
was doomed by a fatal consumption; in September he risked
his life to ride westward through Massachusetts in order to visit
Jerusha, who tended him in his dying days. When Brainerd died
in October, 1747, he became for Edwards even more saintly than
he had been before. Hairne collected and transcribed Brainerd's
meditations and private diary, Edwards published in 1749 *An
Account of the Life of the Late Reverend Mr. David Brainerd,
Minister of the Gospel; Missionary to the Indians.*

The *Memoirs of Brainerd*, as the book afterward became
known, was compiled and produced not merely to celebrate the
life and death of a remarkable man who died at the age of thirty:
Edwards had another purpose in mind, and it was one which was
central in his thought throughout the latter years of his life.[4]
The aim of the *Memoirs* was to declare the power and the actuality of the workings of divine providence in the lives of ordinary
men. It was a subject which Edwards could not treat without the
full scope of a three-hundred-page book and without the realization that he was going directly counter to the opinion of nearly
all his fellow clergymen, even those who had worked valiantly
throughout the Awakening, in asserting the truth of the fact that
human emotions are directions for God's incoming grace. "The
foregoing account of Mr. Brainerd's life," Edwards wrote, "may
afford matter of conviction, that there is indeed such a thing as
true experimental religion, arising from immediate divine influences, supernaturally enlightening and convincing the mind, and
powerfully . . . quickening . . . and governing the heart."[5]

The wonderful "quickening" Edwards had clearly traced
throughout the numerous defenses of the Awakening written
during the earlier years; now he would write, not a defense, but a
triumphant proclamation that these instants of God's incoming

power were quite wholly in accord with those divine prescrip-
tions, those theological ideas, which Edwards had presented and
developed in his youthful ministry. Indeed, the *Memoirs of Brainerd* reminds us that we are back in that vital center of Edwards's
thought out of which had come *God Glorified in Man's Dependence* fifteen or more years in the past. He returned to that doctrine not only because he saw that it had been a true one but
because the passionate and emotional side of Brainerd's life had
been ringed with that splendor of God's light very like what
Edwards himself had known in his own youth. Over and over, in
his comments on Brainerd's self-revelations, Edwards emphasized
the instant, physically felt quality of life. In physical ways Brainerd had known the open arms and the smiling face of Christ; he
had touched and heard the "manifestation of God's glory, and the
beauty of nature, as supremely excellent in itself"; these events
were occasions which marked the way of his conversion, and
they had given him "also a new sense of the infinite wisdom,
suitableness and excellency of the way of salvation by Christ."
This change had been "a great change, and an abiding change,"
which is wrought in true conversions, "rendering him a new man,
a new creature, . . . a change of nature . . . as from corrupt
and dangerous principles in religion, unto the belief of the
truth." [6] In *The Excellency of Christ*, written and preached in
1728, Edwards had outlined the idea which in its varying statements had become a touchstone to his thought: "the glory of
Christ . . . appears to us in excellencies that are of our own
kind, that are exercised in our own way and manner, and so, in
some respects, are peculiarly fitted to invite our acquaintance and
draw our affection. The glory of Christ," Edwards had insisted,
"is brought more to a level with our conceptions, and suitableness
to our nature and manner, yet retaining a semblance of the same
divine beauty, and a savor of the same divine sweetness." [7] The
life of Brainerd was a testament to the truth of this doctrine. For
the effect of the young man's deepening awareness was a strength-
ened conviction of the "doctrines of God's absolute sovereignty"
and "man's universal and entire dependence on God's power and
grace." And so too the "more his religion prevailed in his heart,
. . . the more sensible he was of the certainty and excellency and
importance of these truths, and the more he was affected with
them, and rejoiced in them." The direction of Edwards's argument was clear: he attacked the Arminians and deists who ques-
tioned any affecting emotion and ruled out "that strange and

wonderful transformation of the man" which comes by the actual touches of God's hand in the world, that result in a "renewal of spirit" and bring "heavenly mindedness" and "true Christian morality." [8]

If the *Memoirs of Brainerd* are an affirmation of the depths and vividness of the emotional content of life in the coming of salvation, the book is also fraught with a recognition of the flagging power and loss of feeling which Edwards was knowing in his own life and person. Indeed, the high, challenging rhetoric of the life of Brainerd issued from what Edwards himself had once known and could now look back upon with sadness, yet with joy. Brainerd had duplicated his own experience; the younger man had clearly demonstrated that the single feeling was a resonance of the universe, and that, though God has initiated all things, the instants of apprehension are known in their uniqueness and their divinely given privacy. The *Memoirs* are very like a continuing meditative exercise Edwards had long ago begun in his youth and was to maintain, with increasing vigor, in the latter years of his life. He never stopped exploring his own mind or seeking in the outward manifestations of the physical world these gleaming reflections of God's presence and glory. The memoranda which Edwards jotted and sometimes expanded — some became portions of his sermons — were the teasing moments of speculation caught in the most common or intense hours of daily living and thinking. In this manuscript collection, called *Images or Shadows of Divine Things*, Edwards kept a record of his own mind's workings before and after the years of the Awakening. It is a record of a mind in transition, and it forms a span between Edwards's early mysticism and his later philosophy of the mind and the will.

The diverse jottings which make up *Images or Shadows* seem, at first reading, to turn on a conventional Puritan allegorism. One might think that Edwards's visionary power had so declined, the distance between the object which comes under his scrutiny and the idea he puts down about it on paper has become so great, that the color and shape of the thing have receded into a dim allegorical representation. Take for example such entries as these: "The rising and setting of the sun is a type of the death and resurrection of Christ." "The flame of a candle or lamp," when it burns freshly as it is lit and then goes out when the fire is withdrawn, "seems designed by providence to represent the life of man." [9] Edwards does not see as he once did; the colors of the world are not clear and bright; the shape of objects no longer possesses him; yet the rigors of formal logic and the power of Scriptural analogues still must be heeded. If one read these jottings only to follow Edwards's dying vision, he would find plenty of evidence for any theory he presented: toward the latter part of his life Edwards returned to the chilling requirement that the world be read only as a demonstration of God's eternal types.

The argument might rest there, but it should not. Even if Edwards felt a loss of his responses — what Coleridge nearly a century later would call the failing of his "genial spirits" — and no longer touched the flower or felt the warm sun's ray as he once had, he need not be accused of suffering that waning of his powers which so often makes the latter years of a painter's or a poet's life forlorn. Perhaps Edwards's powers did wane: the intensity of a young man's vision cannot be maintained unswervingly to the end of life. Thought does intrude; speculation does call up the dark ambiguities, whether for Keats after he had stood tiptoe upon a little hill or Thoreau leaving Walden for his life in the village, and men sometimes do live only in the afterglow of their once brilliant powers. The decline of Edwards's power of seeing — that outward- and that inward-looking eye which framed thought along its route of sight — is a part of the man's aging and maturing. Yet, except for the haunting remark in the *Personal Narrative* that his spiritual life did not seem so wondrously clear as it once had been, Edwards never noted that he was aware of the waning of his visionary life. What occurred will take us through *Images or Shadows* and into the later and major writings, the *Treatise Concerning Religious Affections* and the *Freedom of the Will.*

For Edwards, quite obviously, the quality of one's seeing and thinking was a reflection of one's character of mind and spirit. A decaying vision meant a corrupt heart; an eye dull to the world's beauty and to its meanings spelled a private disaster, even a fall, of one's very being. Edwards could reason quite as do modern analysts who see, not divided and differing powers, but the whole design of life which makes a man effective or miserable. Edwards's understanding was not, however, like ours in that it might tend to perform an autopsy on the man's being (the word "being" is out of place in modern descriptive analysis, but since we are considering a man of the eighteenth century, it will serve) and, by arraying all the parts in the design, thereby be able to inform the whole organism. Rather, Edwards and his age saw that the integral parts of a man's being had first to conform to a master plan and then become the seeing, the doing, the believing that are the demonstrations of life. Franklin even supposed that the virtues, thirteen of them to be exact, were first enlivened by his proving that they work and then he could live a prosperous, moral life. That one element in the design was askew did not haunt Franklin, as it might trouble us: the "errata" of life were the very living of life whereby a man grew outwardly from his own self-discovered private center. Not until the Romantic consciousness discovered that a man does not see, live, and believe because he is all of a piece but because he has parts of himself even at desperate war with each other did the grand similitude of consciousness begin to break down. We in our time have learned too well that the discordances and disaffections of life, however painful they are, may be the very impetus to great insight and to heroic work. For Edwards, as for Franklin, this was not so: any aspect, part, or manifestation of being was a disclosure of the whole man; the work, the love, the worship of a man were what the man was.

Yet the ordering of consciousness had its dangers. Not the least was the tendency among many sensitive men of the eighteenth century to reduce the errant vagaries of private experience to master principles, all the while that the surge and stress of one's private life went on its unheeding, unbidden way. The distance can be seen in the Earl of Chesterfield's letters to that absurd, shapeless son, in Boswell's moral cant and in his gusto for living, in Fielding's reduction of Sophia Western to the "idea" Tom Jones can carry with him even when he is absent from her — it will keep the strayed reveller within bounds — and in Hume's annihilative gesture of cause and effect and his history of England as somehow aligned to effect and cause. Edwards risked this danger because, as we shall see, he tended to exalt the Type and the Antitype at the expense of vital experience; he also escaped a submission to the eighteenth-century inconsistency by reason of an insight which may have come to him during the Awakening. Objects in the world, he well knew as early as his studies of the spider and moth, have not only a shape, color, and texture but a tendency, an incentive, a moral directive. In a phrase he restated the idea in *Images:* things of the sense "are lively images of what is spiritual";[10] but that which is "spiritual" is not in the thing seen; it is in the eye and in the character of the beholder. The world is intensely moral: it becomes morally understood only when it is met and matched by an intelligence, a soul, of equal worth and of possible exaltation.

Yet the Type and the Antitype came back, not as sides in an argument, but as appropriate ways of self-inquiry. Edwards considered them in the variety of jottings which he put into his ideas for sermons, into the miscellanies which lurked on the edge of thought, and into these vagrant speculations on the meaning of the world to a single man. "Images" were, for Edwards, the representations of truth — those eternal designs which God has fixed through all time. The "shadows" may have been his own approaches down the long dark ways of consciousness which were still as alive and still as bewildering as they had ever been. Shadows are not wholly dark; they are lit by lights and half-lights, and behind them is the lamp or the sun. Shadows, in Edwards's thought in this time of his life, were those irresolute, wayfaring ideas which teased him into thinking but which never finally yielded up their secret. But what thinking and what thought ever end?

Thus as he considered with himself the decline of spiritual fervor and the implicit failure of his evangelism, he meditated again on the meaning of things to the mind. The opposites in speculation were obviously everywhere: one's self and the world, image and shadow, conversion and damnation, the Book of God and the Book of Nature. The mediation between these opposites was, for Edwards, not some meeting ground halfway between the two; it was not some arbitrarily fixed point wherein, at least abstractly if not really, the differences could be resolved. The mediation was to be for Edwards the mind's activity as, on each new occasion, it found an arc between these disparities. The curve would never be the same: from Scripture to the world was one line; from God to man was another; from substance to thought was still another. If the tracery were honestly done, each moment of thinking and each "image" of divine things would be like nothing ever known before: the arcs would extend from one's self to infinity and back again.

Puritans, it has been tiresomely noted, were caught within a premise, as old as the days of the medieval Schoolmen, that the world of fact was not to be gazed on too fondly; it was full of guile and deceit, and behind it might be the lures to take the soul off to hell. Like so many other historical platitudes, this one has a measure of truth and it does lead us into some moments of appreciation. The New England Puritan was, accordingly, not inclined to speculate or dream about the rose, the willow, and the sunset: if he did so, he must see the shape of God's eternally planted truth behind the gauzy chiaroscuro which nature forever presents to the curious eye. Thus Puritan poetry could seldom inquire into the moment's immediate vision of the commonplace or the strange; and New England versifiers were content for more than a century to remain within the words and phrases given them by the Bible. They could do no more than fashion clumsy redactions of God's pure poetry as set forth in the Psalms and in the visions of the prophets. Mrs. Anne Bradstreet sometimes felt so lost without her husband that she broke through this unquestioned belief about what poetry should be and do; and the Reverend Edward Taylor reverently quibbled over the spinning wheel and the fuller's dye in more ways than testified to their revelations of God's truth behind them.

For the logic of Types was a discipline as rigorous as any in human thought. Even if Scripture and the Book of Nature offered a splendid array of things in order or in opposition and if the Antitypes of God were forever fixed, Edwards could nevertheless find a world of miracle in the idea which came into his mind or the object which caught his eye. To be sure, the age of miracle was long past. No Joshua would ever again make the sun stand still; no voice would speak directly from heaven or from a burning bush and make a man's life go another way. The miracle was to maintain unflinchingly in one's own mind the wonder of thought already known and the equal wonder of thinking yet to be done which the truly religious man finds in God's universe. The outside world might, and does, suffer from that visionary deadness which Edwards had implicitly understood; yet the mind need not decay nor grow sluggish. But how could the wastage of consciousness and of one's daily responses be prevented?

Implicit in the *Images or Shadows* are several ways by which Edwards sedulously brought himself back to the vital purposes of his life. One was that which has marked the ways of poets in recovering something they have lost in their earlier years. When the world of enticing forms begins to pall and one can no longer versify of the flower or the gull in flight, the poet seeks to restore himself by the power of words alone. Words are ministers of the imagination; they can themselves, quite apart from the experience the poet may or may not have had, be the carriers of poetic thought. Indeed, it has been sometimes argued, and with good reason, that the "poetry of experience" is really not of something lived but as of something known in words alone. From Keats to Wallace Stevens and beyond, the imaginative power of words has continually defied the circumstances under which the poet lived and wrote his poetry.

In Edwards the threat of visionary deadness in the latter years was thwarted, at least in part, by a language stratagem which made thinking, any kind of thinking, as vivid as daily experience had been for him in his vibrant youth. Edwards had no need to ride into the woods for refreshment (though he continued a life-long practice of exercise) or sense the changing seasons with the excitement he had once known. The word could conduct him back to the visionary glory he once had known sensuously. It might not be quite the same glory; it was a shining light nonetheless. He could, to put the proposition another way, experience feelingly, deeply, in the word and in the sentence.

He was aided by the discipline of Puritan logic, of the Anti-type and the Type. This ordering of matter and mind was not a lazy way of accepting what other men had offered; it was already a way of meditation which spared the mind a great deal of trouble. It did not do all one's thinking for him; it did some. That "some" was the moral character of any premise or thought. To think, for example, about the ordering of numbers from one to two, to three, to a million, or to infinity is to be submissive to the logical coherence of those numbers in the pattern in which one thinks about them. If one thinks in one's, he is in that prescribed method; if he thinks in two's, he conforms to another requirement; if he ponders the nature of three's (the world's thought displays great energy in the moral management of triangles and trinities), he is of necessity within that frame of speculation. These ways of thought are "moral," therefore, because they have predestined through centuries of speculation that the human mind behave in the orderly fashion of thinking in one's, two's, or infinity. To the extent that all thinking prescribes what is thought, the activity of the mind is painfully, even humiliatingly, circumscribed. Every way of thinking has, to repeat the truism, a moral character. The mind must yield and submit before it can expand and reach.

Words became for Edwards a way of living as clear and vivid as life. They were not a substitute for or a retreat from life; they were a line he could put around a vagary of thought, a speculation, a moment's insight which held that disciplined instant for the next time it might come to mind or be needed. Edwards carefully preserved and even indexed his meditations for the sake of sermons; but these speculative lines he followed were also praises of God, abasements of the self, and prayers let suddenly loose. They might go everywhere; they might die; they were, at the least, expressions of one's own character on the instant of thinking and on the moment of using a word or a phrase. In this way words are the moral links between one's self and a thought. They are versions of most private experience.

At some undated time Edwards wrote in his notebook: "the beautifull cloathing from the silk-worm that the worm yields up at his death represents the glorious clothing we have for our souls by the death of him who became a man, who is a worm and the son of man, who is a worm and who said he was a worm and no man." The syntax is tangled and the rhetoric thorny; the idea may be the accepted trope of dying into life and living into death. The figures appear to be doing the work of thinking as though they had been copied from a book of aphorisms. They also have the fleshly tints of the baroque draftsmen: the worm is the man and yet is he not quite the man who is being devoured and yet lives. The felt ambiguity of mortality and eternity converging in the writhing horror of corruption and decay is finally resolved in the conclusion to the meditation: "And Christ, through exceeding great suffering, yields us his righteousness, that is as fine linnen, clean and white, and presents us without spot to the Father." [11] At the last the penalty is lifted; Christ does care for us, and we are absolved. It would seem that the rhetorical excitement had died away in a mere figure of speech.

Edwards came to live in his mind with a clarity and intensity very like that with which he had once lived in his senses. The excitements of the flesh came to be translated into the delights of language and into the sinuous lines of logic. Less and less Edwards had recourse to analogies to or descriptions of the natural world which tended to fade into a gray monotony; more and more the sheer pursuit of thought, the ferreting out of the idea, and the tracing of an argument in his sermons, his commonplace books, and his formal treatises became for him the necessity of life. He had formerly thought with a pen in his hand; now he seemed to live with the need to record, else the wavering speculation might be forever lost. Language, the word, became for him a way of life and even that possible inclination of man toward God.

3

Edwards often commented on those sensible and natural things which "are lively images of what is spiritual"; the "liveliness" of the image did not depend wholly on whatever incentive it possessed to be known and thought about.[12] The special sensitivity of the perceiver was half of the motion from the thing known to the knower. A man's character, even on the instant of sensing and becoming aware, was vital portion of anything one comes to know. Thus perception was moral, not only because the perceiving induced some moral lesson but because a man brings to every act and to every thought the whole of his being; all his parts act in concert: the ready "affections" which the world allows are not mere exertions by natural law or God's omnipotent power; they are excursions of individual consciousness whose every motion and behavior are summaries of one's total nature.

It is well enough to say, as Emerson would say a century later, that man acts every instant with his whole being and even the twist of his little finger puts to doubt the scoffers and scorners. The main concern is not to affirm the nature of man but to present the ways and the artifices by which man can and should come to any event with his full nature. For a man of Edwards's time and character, the problem was to prove to oneself that one was not suffering from visionary deadness and that, even if one were threatened with a partial loss of sensing and perceiving, one could regain a new and special aptitude, even a new vision. By the mid-1740's Edwards discovered that seeing — the eye's sight of things both as they are and as they appear — was a metaphor of the mind. Light was a configuration of thought on the instant of knowing; the natural light of the sun and the day is not a lure and a deceit, nor is it a mere analogy of the other heavenly light; rather, light is the way by which a thought comes into the mind, and the mind, heeding that bidding, follows the way of thought and thereby comes to know.[13] Edwards saw, therefore, not in colors such as embellish the lines of metaphysical poets; he did not see in clear geometrical shapes whereby men with circles and triangles and squares subsume a world. If he had, then the route of thinking would have come to an end in a set of abstract figures: Emerson curved the universe around a circle, and Thoreau heard history in the whine of wires in the wind. Edwards sought so to keep open the ways of attention that the incoming light always seemed different and the accompanying impression or thought he had was always new. To be sure, no man can continually have a "new" thought; he follows habits of a lifetime; but he can maintain a speculative flexibility by continually forcing himself to test again and again the idea he once had proved true.

Edwards developed a method of thinking in visible pairs. If he could see one idea, he could also see its opposite or its counterpart; and by seeing these two in parallel or in juxtaposition, he could then follow any number of lines outward, downward, or upward. Usually, of course, the way of thought ended: that is, it became resolved in a design, an aphorism, a moral conclusion. But it did so only on that occasion of speculation; over and over Edwards returned to the same idea, almost as if it harassed him, and turned it around and through its sequences of implied or actual pairings. He had to "see" an idea and also "see" its counterpart before he could begin thinking about it. And once he had seen and put down his seeing in words, Edwards could then go on to the ordering of units, pairs, and sequences in the direction of his speculation. An inexact term for this method might be a calculus of algebraic relevances. The entries in *Images or Shadows* display this way of "seeing" thought.

One entry reads, in part: "As the sun, by rising out of darkness and from under the earth, raises the whole world with him, raises mankind out of their beds, and by his light, as it were, renews all things and fetches them up out of darkness, so Christ, rising from the grave and from a state of death . . . raises all his church with him." Here the visible pair, the sun's rising and Christ's rising from the dead, is obvious; each has, however, its own visible extension or pair. The sun's rising each morning is the way by which "all the world is enlightened and brought out of darkness"; so Christ's rising is a sign that "we are begotten again to a lively hope, and all our happiness and life and light and glory and the restitution of all things" come from "his resurrection." [14] The visible pairs are, in another term, a mathematics of spiritual probability. To translate the formula, a would represent the first element and b the second. The continuation of each into another set of pairs would be represented by a^1 and b^1; thus $a:b$ as $a^1:b^1$. The algebraic design can be extended into infinity simply by elaborating and varying the numbers. And since light, as a metaphor of the mind, can be dully or brilliantly refracted into a myriad glints and particles, the calculus of seeing can reach eternity, even, if God allows, to a vision of Himself.

Other entries display this habit of seeing and thinking. Number 60 of the *Images* suggests that the blossoms on a tree in spring, many of which die or are blown down by the wind, are to the coming of ripe fruit as the total numbers of people on earth are to the rollcall of the saved in heaven. Or again, number 61: a raven feeding on dead carrion is to the devil's preying on the souls of the dead in earth as Satan himself relishing the dead "in loathesome putrefaction" who have gone to eternal death. Edwards was not content to establish the algebraic probability: he continued the visionary parallels by noting that "The Devil is the prince of the power of the air, as he is called; devils are spirits of the air. The raven by its blackness represents the prince of darkness. Sin and sorrow and death are all in Scripture represented by darkness or the colour black, but the Devil is the father of sin, a most foul and wicked spirit, and the prince of death and misery." [15] And still again, number 99: a tree with its branches is to the seed or the growing twig from which it grew as the church of God in all its strength now is in contrast to what Christ began. Edwards did not rest with this single pairing of a "lively image": he went on quite clearly to see that in this metaphysical design "There is a marvellous representation of the abundant profusion of God's goodness and lovely grace in what is to be seen in a tree, therein representing what is to be seen in the church. Some particular sorts of trees do more represent the church in some accounts, and others in others, as the vine, the olive, the palm, the apple tree, etc. A tree also is many ways a lively image of a particular Christian with regard to the new man, and is so spoken of in Scripture." [16]

The links and extensions of right pairings can never end. Scripture offers one vast dictionary and nature another of the titles and emblems with which the mind can deal in its reaching toward God. The order of their presentation may be inevitable; Holy Writ reveals no more of its secrets to men today than it did in former centuries, and, though nature may be read more capably in the widening courses of time than it was understood in the ages gone by, yet the mode of its being sensed and known is in the moral character of the man who sees it and whose thought is empowered to follow it in all its diversity. The pairings may be a provisional set of opposites; man's mind is for a moment balanced between these differences of speculation — the sun and the earth, the man and the worm, the sky and the dust particle — but it is allowed the nearly divine privilege of moving into an unending expanse of visionary possibility. Thus even a sentence is a subject with its predicate which together establish a tentative condition; but the sentence is not complete until it has its complements and modifiers. So too a thought is a man's character moving through the infinite range of meaning and speculation of which a word and a sentence are a symbolic artifice, but a true one nonetheless.

Edwards's style takes on a balanced, measured quality which, if one did not search very far, might seem like the most admired syntax of the eighteenth century — phrase on phrase, parallel and contrast in proper order, and the slowly rising thought reaching its syntactical apogee at the end of the sentence. A sentence, like a man's own style of living and thinking, should be a visionary widening; it may begin with a primary grammatical unit of thought, but it foliates into units of images until it has reached its tentative end. The end is, to be sure, only provisional: any sentence may be extended, or it may be succeeded by another sentence which conducts the thought even farther into the broadening terrain of speculation. Edwards kept inserting at the ends of his meditations in *Images* numbers of cross-references to other images whereby a thought once phrased might be embellished or a sentence still to come might already have a beginning even before it was written. Edwards's style obtained measured cadences which were not wholly those practiced in the pulpit or heard in the ear of the exhorting pastor. They were the cadences of a mind dealing with words — and words are mightily resistant things — which could be bound together, not as though just those words were inevitable and necessary for the expression of a thought, but as though the mind were engaged in making those words stand anew. Puritan meditative prose, at its best (and Edwards's is among the best), was very close to Puritan poetry at its best. If the cadences of verse were different from those of prose — a metered argument has a different rhythm from that of a prose argument — they were so only in the compactness of the images and the tensile strength of the lines. Poetry often put the Puritan imagination in chains; prose never did, for if prose were rightly written, then it could reach toward those grace notes of truth with all the facility of man's song. Take, for example, Edward Taylor's stanza from Meditation Ninety-Seven:

> When thou dost shine, a Sunshine day I have:
> When I am cloudy then I finde not thee:
> When thou dost cloud thy face, thy Face I crave.

The Shining of thy face enlivens mee.
I live and dy as Smiles and Frowns take place:
The Life, and Death of Joy Lodge in thy face.[17]

Put with it Edwards's Image numbered ninety-seven:

The beams of the sun can't be scattered, nor the constant stream of their light in the east interrupted or disturbed by the most violent winds here below, which is a lively image of what is true concerning heavenly light communicated from Christ, the sun of righteousness, to the soul. It is not in the power of the storms and changes of the world to destroy that light and comfort. Yea, death itself can have no hold of it.[18]

Taylor's stanza is by any measure very fine; but it suffers from the defect inherent in the thought of "face" and "Face"; it allows both whimsy and reverence because the two are carefully paired and set off against each other. The poet relishes this discord, for he knows that it is not final or real: God's face shines forever above all vicissitudes. Edwards's rumination is similarly a posing of opposites of discord and rest: the light of the sun shines each day as a testament to God's forever-shining light; storms may rage and great changes seem to blot the sun's rays, yet the rays do not flicker. The mode of prose is dispersive, enlarging, even sometimes fragmentary; it reaches no clear determination but ends in dubiety or infinity. The poetic mode of Puritan thought came to rest even at the conclusions of stanzas, for the stanzas were themselves units of thought which, as in the Bay Psalm Book, when "lined out" and sung with the tune and the cadence ending on the dominant chord, were required to be end-stopped. Prose did not obey such rhythmic or cadential laws. The meditative adventure could proceed along ever-widening ranges of paired opposites, of images which called forth other images which, in turn, yielded up still other manifestations of like and unlike. A sentence could be, as it was for Edwards, a unit of time suspended between past and present, for even the occasions of past and present were the pairing of speculative opposites. Time became very often a conditional present wherein just those relevances and syntactical possibilities were framed and from which a further speculation might appear. For example:

The blue colour of the serene skie, which is a pure, pleasant colour, yet is a feeble colour: it is by a reflection of the weakest and least rays of the sun's light, hereby representing admirably not only the purity of the happiness of the saints in heaven, but that blessed humility and as it were holy pusilanimity that they are of.[19]

The present condition of the "serene skie" is posed against the present state of the saints in heaven and the future possibility of the sanctified on the earth. Time itself becomes a way of speculation, and the temporal ways of words allow for openness and diversity. One can range through syntactical occasions almost as if he were allowed to roam at will through the history of man. Thus, if one is bound to a narrow space of thinking, one's mind is allowed to venture far, even limitlessly, along the way which words alone permit.

Even as Edwards's ministry contracted with the waning of the Awakening and his hold on his parishioners weakened until he was finally removed from his pastorate, and even as the range of daily living narrowed, Edwards's mind in middle life opened and broadened. And as he became more and more convinced of the fated character of life and as he put tighter lines and boundaries to his own speculation, Edwards adventured farther into language and the deeper implications of thought, and thereby he enlivened his own mind. What outwardly seemed so predestined and closed now became a new openness within his own mind; and even if the very words he used bore with them the inevitable meanings God from the beginning had intended them to have, he came to see that those words were the tools of the intellect and the proper vestiges of the soul. Edwards reached a position in his private thought which ended, apparently, in a paradox: language is predisposed to be just what it is; no word can be or mean anything except what God intended; a sentence is a locution of thought which must be just that sentence with its subject, predicate, and complements. Yet language is a way of vision: if the word "blue" is, as Edwards wrote, "a feeble colour" derived by reflection from "the sun's light," it is also a perception sustained and known in the mind even when there is nothing blue to be known. The mind need not have the mere sensings of things; thinking and understanding can go their way led by the "light within." Thus, if words seem to serve the uses of men in their daily living and even if they mean in their time only what God and human culture require them to mean, words are nevertheless measures of man's moral being and a society's character. Men think and they speak because they must; yet language is a key to spiritual growth and to spiritual decay. Any man, if he seeks to learn for himself, can trace through his thought the way by which he came to believe and to live by the finest perceptions and convictions of his life.

4

The entries in the record known as *Images or Shadows* deepened and intensified as the Awakening came and then passed away; in their scattered probings at the heart of belief and at the basis of his own life, these jottings constitute a remarkable testament to the stress and the power, as well as the weakening, which Edwards could sense and trace throughout his life. Yet during the Awakening Edwards set down another record, a document in his most private history which attempted to detail for his own speculation what the narratives of Phebe Bartlet and others had done for the world outside. It was left a fragment at Edwards's death and was published long afterward under the commonplace title of *Personal Narrative*.[20] It is one of the most memorable pieces of religious autobiography ever written, standing beside *The Little Flowers of St. Francis* or the *Apologia pro Vita Sua of* Cardinal Newman.

In its way the *Personal Narrative* is a dark and tragic work. It reveals, albeit in terms and twists of thought particular to Edwards and to an ecclesiastical mind, a profound sense of the loss of what had been so important in Edwards's youth — the loss of physical awareness of God's wondrous world. Even as he is boastfully proud of the response he always has to the Word and to those occasions when God becomes known to men, he becomes aware that the world of natural forms grows increasingly remote from him and resistant to his thought. The senses become dull; the fires of wonder and poetic response become banked, and, as the middle years of his life and the dramatic days of the Awakening passed by, Edwards came to know that visionary deadness which is the tragedy not only of a poet but of a seer and a mystic. To lose that sense of delight of his earlier years was, for Edwards, the danger of losing at least half of the possible understanding of God and His universe. The *Personal Narrative* is, accordingly, a document in a most sensitive man's loss of joy and wonder — and, as well, that man's recovery.

The transitions and shifts in Edwards's responses to the natural world are difficult for a modern reader to trace and appreciate. A later time is accustomed to having these private disclosures couched in a rhetoric, a vocabulary, which has become an accepted, even a drearily monotonous, mode of self-revelation. We are quite well aware of the narrative of a sensitive, suffering youth issuing all unprepared into the world and undergoing those travails of flesh and spirit which form the *Bildungsroman* of modern consciousness. Edwards did not provide such an outline nor use an accustomed rhetoric; indeed, the curiosity of the *Narrative* is that, from the earliest to the latest records of his mind, the vocabulary changes hardly at all. He could narrate the inward sensings of his mature years in just the same terms in which he had presented the excitements of his youth. On a "Saturday night, (*January*, 1739) I had," he wrote, "such a sense, how sweet and blessed a thing it was to walk in the way of duty; to do that which was right and meet to be done, and agreeable to the holy mind of God; that it caused me to break forth into a kind of loud weeping, which held me some time, so that I was forced to shut myself up, and fasten the doors." He could still "see" as clearly as he ever had; the sight was, however, not of outward things but wholly within the mind. "It appeared to me a great clog and burden," Edwards confessed, "that what I felt within, I could not express as I desired. The inward ardor of my soul, seemed to be hindered and pent up, and could not freely flame out as it would." [21] What a modern reader misses or misconstrues in the *Narrative* is the sense of struggle: there is none. No more than Emerson, who suffered a similar visionary loss, was Edwards able to draw the reasons why such an event had taken place in his life; yet in the course of fifteen or twenty years the change of a lifetime had occurred. For some like Thoreau and Kierkegaard it is a nightmare journey; for others it is the necessary, the endurable distance one travels, not because one wishes to do so nor because the fated loss of sensibility is part of life's pain, but because God has meant a man to move from the wonders of the senses to the greater wonder of his mind. Edwards came to realize that a man can live very well, even faithfully as God intends, within his mind alone.

The *Narrative* turns on a question which had already tinged Edwards's thought and which was to haunt him the rest of his life; it would not be resolved (if it could ever be answered) until the *Freedom of the Will*, written more than a dozen years afterward. It was the question of Cause — God's cause and the world's causation and their relation to a man's will. In reviewing his life,

Edwards realized and traced out in luminous detail that the occasions of incoming grace had, in his early years, come almost wholly from outside his own being. He in himself had in no wise been a "cause"; the swelling and then the diminishing awareness of God's power and His perpetual grace had come like the movement of minute particles of causation in a Newtonian world; and what had brought about the declining sense of God's nearness had been the decline in Edwards's own responses. To lose the feeling of wonder in the earth, the air, the sunlight was awesome enough; but to lose the soul's sensing of God's holiness because one's physical responses were waning was even more terrible. Could he have erred in fixing his faith in God's presence on the immediacy of physical things? In a moment of anxiety recollected long after its occasion, Edwards noted: "it is affecting to think, how ignorant I was, when a young Christian, of the bottomless, infinite depths of wickedness, pride, hypocrisy and deceit, left in my heart." When others came to him and spoke of "their longing to be 'humbled to the dust,'" he wondered if their admission of despicableness had any relevance to the true state of their souls. However suitable "their degrees of humility" might be as they confessed their heinousness, he came to see that the very act of humiliation might be "a vile self-exaltation." What made the occasion of a minister's hearing the admissions of sin from his parishioners even less trustworthy was that the "vile self-exaltation" might be not only the parishioner's but the minister's.[22] A clergyman could become so engrossed in the confessions of his flock, of the saved even as of the damned, that he might well assume that all the abasement of the flesh and the shrieks of the tormented souls were meant only for his enlightenment and delectation. A minister could become ever more vile than the lowest of his flock — a conclusion which Edwards anticipated more than a hundred years before Hawthorne would give it its classic treatment in *The Scarlet Letter*. Edwards came therefore to distrust the manifold testimony of the senses and the fleshly living of man as the true demonstration of a man's way of lying "infinitely low before God." The world is not all a cheat; it cannot be so, for it is of God. Yet the actions of the senses may become so habitual and commonplace that one can very well be dead to what still is and always will be so very much alive. The deadness may be in that strange midway region between feeling and thought and may lie somewhere along the route Locke had traced from the acts of nature to the motions of the mind.

Edwards had a name for this power which lies in the outside world and makes itself felt in the human mind; he had used it often before. It was God's "sovereignty" — the cognitive route of all our sensing and thinking which move, not in madness or disorder, but in a known, apprehensible order: the very flow of our ideas discloses that there is an intelligence behind everything felt and known. Thus, in the *Personal Narrative*, Edwards came back to that theological principle of the days of his earliest sermons and *God Glorified in Man's Dependence* and was again assured that "God's absolute sovereignty and justice, with respect to salvation and damnation, is what my mind seems to rest assured of, as much as of any thing that I see with my eyes." And again he stressed in his autobiography that "The doctrines of God's absolute sovereignty . . . and man's absolute dependence on the operations of God's Holy Spirit, have very often appeared to me as sweet and glorious doctrines." [23]

Thus to live in submission is to live in divine wonder. And thus for Edwards the character of a man is not really his own and certainly not of his making. Indeed, character became Edwards's equivalent of the Puritan doctrine of predestination: just as we were given the outward world in which to live, so we are allowed to think with that mind God has given us; the route of thinking and the way of the soul's understanding are as well prescribed as are the motions of atoms.

Yet God's sovereignty was forever opposed by man's will, which subverted the data of the senses, the cognitions of the mind, and even the manifestations of men's abasement and confession to its own low selfish requirements. If the mind and the soul could free themselves of the galling demands of pride, the world's praise, the lure of power, and the indomitable demands of self-realization, then mind and soul might be able to look within and see the truth of God's "holiness" and from thence a man's true being. The will forever got in the way; it acted like a third power midway between flesh and spirit. It was another voice, the sound of the cheating knavery of pride and of spiritual sloth. Edwards could not subvert and renounce the will; he had to live with it, just as he had to live with his five senses; but he could see how fallible it was: it was neither bound to mere sensual existence nor leagued to the mind's apprehensions. It was the point at which the opposing self dared to affirm its single being in despite of all that science and right teaching declared. Thus, not so much by abnegation, prayer, and withdrawal did Edwards seek to bring the will into subjection; rather, he turned to intellectualizing the sense of things and the ideas in the mind. The young man's responses to the world had dimmed; yet the will seemed as active as it had ever been; only thinking, and thinking ever more rigorously, would serve to awaken Edwards from that visionary deadness in which he had found himself.

At the very end of the *Personal Narrative* he wrote: "I had . . . a very affecting sense, how meet and suitable it was that God should govern the world, and order all things according to his own pleasure; and I rejoiced in it, that God reigned, and that his will was done." [24] The autobiographical record was but a fragment, but it poised life between the two ways a man's life may go — between the glory of the world and that other glory of the intellect and mind where a man may live alone and perhaps find himself again. The problem of cause and the will had been posed; the succeeding thought and the next writings would undertake the further quest.

7

The Will and the Mind

IN THE year 1749 the troubles in the Northampton parish increased. Edwards would not abandon his demand that the applicant for admission to the church be examined concerning the state of his soul. In the eyes of his parishioners the issue seemed the worst form of ecclesiastical aristocracy and even tyranny: the history of the reformed churches in America for nearly a century and a half had been a movement, if not toward latitudinarianism, at least in the direction of God's manifesting Himself both in His word and in the world He had made. New England might be charged with leaning toward an amiable, even an heretical deism; in Edwards's church the issue was more simply stated: it was that Edwards was revoking a privilege which his noble grandfather had instituted and which he himself had followed for twenty-three years. Indeed, it seemed to many in Northampton that the minister was reviving a long-dead issue either out of private pique or out of some inexplicable necessity.[1]

Edwards sought to put the issue on the highest spiritual level of debate. He obtained the permission of the church to declare that a state of controversy existed between the minister and people. With all the learning in Scripture and theology he could muster, he patiently set forth his reasons in a treatise entitled *An Humble Inquiry into the Rules of the Word of God, Concerning the Qualifications Requisite to a Compleat Standing and Full Communion in the Visible Christian Church*, published in the early autumn of 1749. The issue was, quite plainly, that Edwards required for admission into the fellowship of the church more than a mere "profession" and its subsequent approval by the minister and elders that the confessor lived a good life. He acknowledged that salvation was indeed an inward "renovation of the heart" and that any human test was inadequate, as the years of the Awakening had borne witness, to discover the depth of the change of spirit in one who asked to be admitted to full communion. Edwards nevertheless reaffirmed that the sacrament of the Lord's Supper was given only to those who had truly professed and who truly

believed. All the others might be in the church, but they were out-
siders and not communicants.

To a modern reader *An Humble Inquiry* is painstaking in its
logic and tedious in the unrelenting proofs of its argument. Edwards was insisting on the established truths of the New England
churches as those principles had been set forth in the councils of
the ministers and in the Platforms of the seventeenth century.
That the people of his church and of the community had lost
touch with those doctrines made Edwards's task of suasion and
proof all the more difficult; and that he failed — only twenty
copies of the treatise were distributed in the town, and most of
those went unread — was apparent when Edwards preached a
series of five sermons in March, 1750, and few of his opponents
troubled even to come and hear him. A Council of the elders of
the church was called and was convened on June 19; the outcome
was inevitable. After three days' debate the Council on June 22
voted to sever the ties between the minister and the church. On
July 2 Edwards stood in the pulpit of his church and delivered his
Farewell Sermon. It was among his most distinguished utterances.
His burden in the first part was to show that, however effectively
a minister may be separated from his parishioners here on earth,
they will have to stand together at the Last Judgment when all
strife and bickering will have ceased and the truth will be forever
clear. Edwards was treating a subject which had been with him
since his youth: this earth is but a way station and a cloudy
"image" of the great things God will reveal in His good time. Yet
Edwards spoke without rancor: God, the "great Judge," will
"declare what is right . . . , approving him that has been just and
faithful, and condemning the unjust." Ministers and people will
alike stand together in that awful day. Edwards then proceeded
to remark that his leaving was "in some respects in a peculiar
manner a melancholy parting" chiefly because his teachings had
"served no other purpose" than apparently to harden their hearts
against him. Even so, he could not leave them without his cau-
tions: he addressed the various groups in the church — people he
had known all their lives, the children and the young folk, and he
especially cautioned that the home be kept the sacred place for
"the maintaining of *family order*." He closed with the hope that
he "be remembered in the prayers of all God's people that are of
a calm spirit, and are peaceable and faithful in Israel." [2]

Edwards remained in Northampton until he received a call to
be minister to the church in Stockbridge and missionary to the

Indians. He journeyed to that village on the edge of the wilderness, inspected the house provided for his family, and then entered upon his duties there in the summer of 1751. The place, despite its remoteness and its rudimentary conditions of living, had its advantages: it offered Edwards a solitude and a chance to return to his study which he had perforce virtually abandoned throughout the difficult times in Northampton. Here, for three years, he would consider the ideas of a lifetime and produce his masterwork.

Some men who pass through great occasions in their lives and then come out on the hither side may be nostalgic, remorseful, or arrogant. The curiosity of Edwards in defeat and in exile — Stockbridge was a virtual exile for a minister who had played so prominent a role as Edwards had played — was that his mind was emboldened not only to return to the old adventure of his ideas but to undertaken new speculations. Thus Edwards lived his remaining years (he would have seven of them) uncomplaining and unprotesting. The reason was not a docility of spirit: Edwards could be an oppressively arrogant man; the reason was that Edwards had been so long accustomed to living within his own mind that the acceptance of a bleaker life on the Massachusetts frontier of Stockbridge was a new freedom to do what he felt he was intended to do and to become again what he had been earlier in those memorable days of his early pastorate. He would find again the courses of his thought, and he would not be deflected by petty arguments or angry disputation. He sought, perhaps all unaware of what he was doing, to complete the autobiography of his own mind. In two writings, separated by eight years, he undertook the way his thought had destined him to go; he returned to that central and plaguing question of the eighteenth century: Is life and is thought open to all the impelling directions which, so strangely, they seem to follow, or are they bound within a limitation so narrow that the merest motion is required and nothing comes about except as it was meant absolutely to be? The question was more than a renewal of the argument of the age: it was a necessity for Edwards himself to seek an answer, else his own life was meaningless circumstance and all that he had sought to do but the direction of brute atoms. The first of two writings to explore this question is the *Treatise Concerning Religious Affections*, which, though it was published in 1746 before Edward's removal from his church, is a companion piece to the *Freedom of the Will*.

The *Treatise* attempted to describe the "nature" of the affections and "Their Importance in Religion." The term "nature" suggests an anatomy — a division of the affections into their constituent elements. But because affections are feelings, they are not subject to the same methods of analysis and description as are natural objects. Nevertheless, religious affections have a "nature," and they effect "common and saving operations," which must be distinguished from those "subjects . . . which are not of a saving nature." In the first part of the *Treatise* Edwards described what constitutes true religious affections; they are "all the faculties and principles of the human soul" which tend toward "the great business for which God has created [man], that is the business of religion." In the second part Edwards entered upon an analysis of "signs": since his age had looked for and had found so many approved ways by which religious belief could be supported, Edwards showed that there "are no certain signs that religious affections are truly gracious, and that they are not." Then, in the third part, Edwards undertook to show that there are twelve true and "distinguishable signs" of holy affections. In the end he returned to the well-tested doctrine of justification long ago set forth by Paul: justification was achieved by Christ's death and resurrection; man's redemption is still a matter of hope in the future, for the demonic powers are still alive and active. Yet man need not wait until the triumph of Christ at the end of the world in order to gain justification: for Edwards "we are justified by the righteousness of Christ" in this age and in our lifetime.

The *Treatise* is deceptive. It seems to use one form of logic in order to reach a contrary conclusion: it assumes a brute, mechanistic universe — and proves the spiritual autonomy of God. It proposes that God is a mechanistic-mathematical unity to which all parts of the universe precisely conform — and it restores the immediacy of God in the instant activity of His universe. The reason for this paradoxical posing of arguments was that Edwards could not use Platonic or Berkeleyan idealism in order to counter a system, the prevailing one of his day, which made ideas conform to the sensory route from impulse to thought; Berkeley had disposed of the age's mechanism by locating everything, not in the world, but in the mind. What the mind knows, is; and what the mind perceives as "real" is a true projection of itself. Edwards had to remain within the accredited assumptions of his time: he could not brush aside the stone as an immaterial object simply because the mind knows it immaterially; and he could not make the stone something truly real because it had had an antecedent reality long before any man had known it. The mind and its thought may be bound — and they may be free: an honest inquirer must establish his freedom or bondage for himself. A life which is wholly bound to circumstance can hardly be known, much less saved; and a life which is free, really free, can know anything and be saved at will. Somewhere between the two positions the truth might lie. Edwards brought a lifetime's thought to the question.

In the *Treatise* Edwards offered a suggestion he would elaborate in *Freedom of the Will:* God's knowledge and the world's history are comformable to God alone. God had initiated the Covenant for purposes of His own and beyond the knowing of men; it was not devised for man's comfort and benefit even if, by its terms, man might be saved. Yet God did covenant with His people that He would bestow on them more than they could have and more than they deserved of themselves. To be sure, His divine goodness is a self-operating principle and not shared with men; it belongs only to Him. Yet God did so agree to bestow His grace; by so agreeing He became not wholly a free will. Indeed, He became less than His godhead and thereby ordained that His will would be free only within those self-determining limitations. This self-limiting will is forever revealed in nature and in human life: nature's laws disclose "tendencies," and human life is the subject of "affections" which God manifests among His children. The two forces are really not separate: God has so limited Himself that the tendencies He reveals in the world conjoin exactly with the "affections" men are capable of feeling and knowing; God never exerts a force which is not held within the confines of His own will and within the limited power of man's intelligence. " 'Tis also undoubtedly true," Edwards reasoned, "that the Spirit of God is very various in the manner and circumstances of his operations, and that sometimes he operates in a way more secret and gradual, and from smaller beginnings, than at others." God's power is "entirely different from and beyond our power," and, as Edwards continued with his rather thorny rhetoric, "above the power of nature. . . . Certainly it is in no wise unreasonable to suppose that this effect" of God's power "should very frequently be produced after such a manner, as to make it very manifest, apparent, and sensible that it is "the power of God and not that of man.[3]

By means of this argument of God's self-imposed limitation,

Edwards raised the question central to a man's private life-history: Is any natural, physical experience a sign of God's inclining? The answer was, quite obviously, It is not. Some acts of nature may never touch the mind and the soul; contrariwise, men may be deeply moved by motions of the mind while the body is outwardly unaffected. The mind and the soul need not concur in the actions of the body; "there is a sensation of the mind," Edwards said, "which loves and rejoices, that is antecedent to any effects on . . . the body; and this sensation of the mind, therefore, don't depend on these motions in the body, and so may be in the soul without the body." [4]

Here, for Edwards, was once more a meeting of Locke's thought and the doctrine of the Covenant: even though the mind and the soul are not free to act and think apart from the data of the senses, yet the mind and the soul are not mechanistically bound by mere reality. Locke's idea of "power" — objects in nature make impressions quite apart from the physical order and even the behavior of their constituent particles — Edwards translated into his theory of nature's "tendency." "Tendency" is that ageless force and direction which God has intended the world to follow. Atoms conform to their route of behavior because of just that "tendency" God has intended them to have. Not all atoms follow the same route: a stone makes a differing impression on different men, not simply because one man's sensitivity is dull or keen, but because God has determined — always within those foreordained limitations He disposed in the beginning — that each moment's impression is different from all other moments. Every instant of sense is the fusing of nature's "tendency" and man's responding "affection"; the calculus of potential variety is infinite.

Thus Edwards in these latter years returned to the Covenant and even to the Lockean principles of sensation in order to restore the content and the validity of single, living consciousness. Sensing and thinking are, therefore, not isolated units in a sequence of acts called mental cognition: they are what man has as the beginning of self-inquiry, for man must hunger and thirst, yearn and despair, not merely that he may continue to live but that he may know. Man builds his world from within and, once having built that world, he lives there the rest of his days.

The *Treatise Concerning Religious Affections*, coming as it did shortly after the end of the Awakening, marked Edwards's meditative pause as he sought to sustain himself in the dark hours of failure. He was daily beset by the controversy in his parish which threatened to destroy his very peace of mind; and the aftermaths of the great conversions revealed that the seed of the Word had many times fallen on very thin and unprosperous ground. Quite apparently God had not heeded the cries or opened His way to the chief of sinners. The *Treatise* was, therefore, a narrative of Edwards's mind seeking to discover why God had not fulfilled His purposes, at least as those purposes had loomed so brightly a mere four or five years before. The *Treatise* is, however, more than a mournful epilogue to the Awakening. It has none of the angry disputatiousnesss of the defenses of that movement, and it relies on none of the evidence, human or spectral, which burdened the *Narrative of the Surprising Conversions*. It breathes a sweet reasonableness because Edwards had already resigned himself to admitting that God's ways among men are past knowing; the best one can search out and perhaps find are God's ways with one's self. The book is, furthermore, marked by a deeply pious man's humility in the face of his littleness: it is as though Edwards were returning to the days of his own awakening wherein he saw his abject triviality in the awesome might of God's universe and his own evil appeared mountainous like "Infinite" heaped "upon infinite."

Yet a man could not truly be born again, not in the middle or declining years of his life. If conversion had once come, it had come forever; one's foot might slide in due time, but one regained one's spiritual composure by ways other than self-abasement, a return to the springs of one's being, or nostalgia for times of enlightenment which never come again. Edwards could no more have found his place in God's universe after the terrible occasions of the Awakening than he could have become a child again and entered the rudely built hut he and his friends had used for prayer; and he could not regain the spiritual wonder which had been his in New York or at the beginning of his ministry. A man's intellect is his very special possession; it is one of God's great talents which it would be an even duller spiritual death to hide than if it were used simply to cast up one's accounts and set the record aright in the eyes of men and God.

With the *Treatise Concerning Religious Affections* Edwards virtually abandoned history, his own and mankind's, because he had come to realize that history was fraught with danger. It lured men to the conviction that they lived at the very peak of time, albeit their decades were hardly worth scrutiny in the narrative of God; it also teased men into believing that the eternal types of God could be seen as readily now as yesterday, whereas the antitypes, being God's manifestations, are changeless and accordingly unknown. History was especially beguiling, and therefore suspect, because the earthly, sensible manifestations of God whereby man could feel and apprehend were not along a causative way like the march of centuries. What man apprehended from dawn to ruddy sunset was an intricate, ever-various "tendency" which, from hour to hour, offered some new disposition, a fresh insight. Edwards could not restore the vitality, much less the content, of that original inspiriting excitement he had known in his young manhood: the woods would never breathe in quite the same way again, and he would not again fall on his face in terror and wonder as he several times had. What he could affirm was the mercurial intensity, the still quick vitality of his intellect, and the possibility of knowing God even more fully than he had when his senses and his mind had been awake to impressions. If the intellect were the way, then it too must be humbled in order that it may rise; the mind would seek its limitations and then it might come anew and well to a knowledge of God. In his masterwork, *A Careful and Strict Inquiry into the Modern Prevailing Notions of That Freedom of Will*, published in 1754, Edwards undertook a full disclosure of these ideas.

2

Freedom of the Will (to give the book its convenient and shorter title) remains to this day a rare and awesome treatment of a subject which, even as soon as it was published, had very little interest for readers of its time but which, in our own decades of the twentieth century, is gaining numbers of respectful students. As a masterly treatment of its subject, it can be set beside such diverse books as Horace Bushnell's *God in Christ*, C. S. Peirce's five essays which were seminal to Pragmatism, William James's *Will to Believe*, and G. E. Moore's *Principia Ethica*. It is, however, quite different from these works: while they nearly all adventured into daring and new ranges of speculation and even, in several instances, ushered in a quite radical approach to moral thought, Edwards's masterpiece had no successors; indeed, *Freedom of the Will* treated ethical principles in a way in which no serious student had approached them for a century. It set out to be a massive assault on Arminianism — the view that God stands ever ready to receive the repentant sinner and that, speaking generally, man can save himself — and it came upon a time when nearly all good Christians were, in one way or another, fully convinced Arminians. It was as if someone today were to revive the old notion of man's "moral sense," a functioning organ which can be located in the human cranial cavity, and by reviving a discredited anatomical theory, produce a brilliant and contemporary moral inquiry. For the implications of *Freedom of the Will*, its range of argument, its mastery of ideas, and its remorseless logic, take it far beyond the narrow confines of an antique heresy or the outworn cant of Puritan theology.

By the time he had finished writing the defenses of the Awakening and was looking inward upon his own conscience and soul in *A Treatise Concerning Religious Affections*, Edwards found himself in the same dilemma as other eighteenth-century philosophers and theologians: he had reduced human thinking and the idea of the will to the status of but another expression of natural energy in the world. He had well reasoned that cognition is a faculty lodged in the mind; knowing is in ever-effective concord with the daily activity of the cosmos. Man is not some unique being but is another creature responding sensibly, rationally, to the "tendencies" of his world and moving through his life by means of the "affections" which he feels and organizes into habits and ways of life. Edwards still had to answer the question left over from Newtonian physics and Lockean epistemology; it could be stated as follows: If man has mind and will and if these faculties are inextricably bound to the activity of the real and the phenomenal worlds, then how can a human will function in a universe of matter, of implacable cause and effect, wherein no evidence can be found for a law or principle of will? How, in other words, can man's will be distinguished from laws of nature which do not act as "wills" but which behave according to laws they are powerless to alter? How can the will, whether free or limited, be released from what Edwards called "the ghastly hold of reality"?

This question could not be answered by any principle such as Locke's sensation and reflection, or even "power." If it could, then man has no will: to have a will he would be able to will for or against even those ideas which are already in the mind before any act of willing takes place. A necessitarian skeptic like Hume sought to support some basis for human will by transcending mere sense psychology: the will was, for Hume, that aggregate of thought which did seem to have direction toward ends in life and which served the human animal in its chances for survival. A nominalist like Berkeley found enough evidence for the will in the very words "will" and "willing": if man had the names he must have the ability on which the words rest.

Edwards's argument for the will as well as his attack on the illusion of the will as free is one of the most brilliant and devastating in intellectual history. Since the reasoning depends on a set of principles which were at least sixty years old when he published the book, we might, rather than investigate Edwards's treatise, begin with Newton and that World-as-Machine which Newtonian thought seemed to support by the mid-eighteenth century.

The theory of gravitation was an hypothesis based on the infinite recurrence of similar events; an atom, a ball, a particle of dust, a shooting star, a planet, indeed everything that had the character of motion behaved throughout all time in accordance with an immutable principle — the "law" of motion. Furthermore, no matter where one looks, the same law seems to obtain in varying and measurable degrees of intensity: a lead pellet falls much faster than does a feather; yet both move and fall. Nevertheless, Newton rejected a purely mechanistic theory of the world because laws of matter in motion, even as they are observed and recorded, may not be the true "laws" which move those objects; they may indeed be reflections of still other laws or principles of motion. Substances do not make their own laws and move themselves: the stone dislodged from the precipice fell, not because it contained its own theory of plummeting into the valley, but because it was acting in accordance with force and motion long antecedent to its being on the precipice's edge. Evidence neither from matter nor from human experience supported a rigid, logical cause-and-effect explanation for the behavior of the world. The theory of gravitation was, therefore, a mathematical formula, a descriptive, symbolic abstraction; it was an approximation, not necessarily the truth, of activity which seems to be going on everywhere in the universe. To suppose that gravitation is a law, eternal and invariable in all atoms of the cosmos, was, for Newton, to assert the most errant fallacy. The gravitational theorem was propounded at a time when, apparently, human inquiry into natural phenomena could go no further than such a principle allowed. Afterward, in the course of generations, other theorems, even other laws, would have superior claims and thus come to supplant this one. In the present state of knowledge Newton admitted that gravity is the best, though provisional, statement man has to describe matter in motion.[5]

No one could say, however, that gravity denies will. An object moving through space is not making its own motion; it was directed by a force long before it began its journey. Nor, on the other hand, does gravity prove will; it is not itself an act of "willing," for it conforms to some principle larger than and outside itself. Gravity may have no more will than the stone it unseats and drops into the valley. For Newton, accordingly, neither is the universe a will or is it mechanistically "willed" from somewhere outside itself; gravity is simply a power, a function, a descriptive metaphor whereby man may know better than he formerly knew what the universe is doing. It need not be forever true nor is it likely to be demonstrably proved in all the minutiae of the cosmos.

Because of the enormous and popular hold which Newtonian thought gained over men's minds, the eighteenth century committed itself to finding relationships between laws of nature and laws of the human mind. If, as many reasoned, the mind functions in the world of matter, derives its images and ideas from that world, and goes through its span of existence in conformity with myriads of other objects in space and motion, then it can have no idea except those which objects in space and time give it. If, on the other hand, the mind is able to think quite on its own, to originate and sustain ideas apart from the data of sense and each hour's living, then it is presumably not bound to matter in motion; it is free. On these issues the eighteenth century expended some of its best intellectual effort; theorists rose in order to support or counter the moral analogies to the theory of gravitation. Shaftesbury's idea of morality as some ultimate aesthetic form far outside the observed behavior of atoms and men; Mandeville's principle of use and consumption as a law of ethical conduct; and the notions of the Scottish moralists who saw the human psyche conform to the twin directions of pleasure and pain — these were the doctrines which were caught between a brute moral necessitarianism (things are because they must forever be what they are), from which ethical philosophers sought every means of escape, and a moral freedom (things are because they conform to an intention and plan higher than themselves), which they sought every means of proving.

Even in their most rigorous exercises of the intellect to define or limit the will, speculative men never doubted that something like a "will" did exist. If man were an animal who has the power of thought, then he must have some control over what he is thinking about; sense psychologists who derived from Locke were troubled because the route of cognition, from mere sense impression to ideas in the mind, reduced the will to be only a minor function of the mind which sifts out those impressions it will accept and rejects those which it prefers not to consider; and the supporters of the pleasure-pain theory could locate a will in that antecedent power which determines what a human being will find pleasurable and what he will know as painful. That man was a mere automaton was inconceivable even to a century which put much faith in the universe as a machine and its god as a divine mechanic: somehow a principle of the will — and, what is more, the will as free — had to be located even in a universe of jarring matter and immutable law. Indeed, the major effort of the age was not to prove the existence of the will — obviously man, to be a man at all, had to have a will just as he had the power of speech — but to support the freedom of the will even in an apparently will-less universe. Some, like Hume and Adam Smith, sought a basis for human will by transcending mere sense psychology: "will" is not, they argued, a form of thought; it is a separate human power.[6] Arminians like Clarke and Whitby, whom Edwards strenuously opposed, reasoned that the will was God's special gift to man in order to rectify, even if partially, the awful damage wrought by our first parents' loss of innocence.[7]

Edwards's attack was not on the theory that man has a will; man is a child of God and thus, no matter how debased he may become, has some portion of God's power latent in him. Rather, Edwards's attack was on the "prevailing notion" that the will is a free, operative agent and that each man, from his first to his last hour, can direct not only his acts of choice but his reasoning which will in turn produce those next acts of choice. Edwards's attack was one of the most devastating in intellectual history; for purposes of convenience I have arranged the stages of this attack in an arbitrary order and given them italicized headings.

The "Consensus Gentium." For centuries men have argued that the human will makes decisions in accordance with principles which inhere in that well-used phrase "common sense." That aggregate sense which men share with other men to do one thing and to avoid another has resulted, throughout the span of many centuries, in an accepted judgment concerning what is good and bad, useful and wasteful. Thus, almost without his knowing, man does good or evil as he is pulled by his wishes, desires, temptations, and his society because he is the inheritor of infinite acts of judgment and choice all of which together have supplied him with what he can simply take for granted as his own and as other men's as well, namely "common sense." Men do not go counter to common sense because, throughout ages, they have learned better; and while some men do misbehave and bring trouble into the world, they are deviants from the normal way; they are punished, correct themselves, and thereby see the truth of moral common sense, or else, like idiots and unregenerate criminals, they are outside the bounds of decent human society.

This argument is based in several assumptions, both of which Edwards undertook to discredit. One is the appeal to the logic of dissimilarity or to the opposites of moral speculation. The reasoning goes something as follows: If A is free and B is not free, then any combination of A plus B is both free and not free at the same time; A and B are free and not free to the extent that their "natures," as Edwards called them, are joined to form that connection. Therefore, A is free and B is not free (or, conversely, A is not free and B is free) because all that they have ever been — their characters, their situations, and their fundamental "natures" — has predisposed them to be and to act in varying degrees and kinds of freedom. To suppose that each instant of acting and choosing for A and for B has its own special, recognizable character and degree of freedom is to do violence to the known content of any event: someone is free to the extent that he acts in a free manner in one situation, and he is not free to the degree that he cannot act freely in another situation.[8]

Edwards reduced the theory of the *consensus gentium* to nonsense by means of a linguistic argument. He posed "common sense" against the absurd. According to this logic, any statement contains three parts: it is a statement; it supposes, because it is a statement, its own contradiction; and it ends on a resolution or proof — or, it may be, in an absurdity. Thus any statement, with its subject, its predicate, its object and complements, is a mode of experience presented and known at the moment of one's hearing, reading, and apprehending that statement. A sentence is not, therefore, a fictitious approximation to something known, a various and circuitous approach; words are, to rephrase the idea in "Sinners in the Hands of an Angry God," real adventures along a real pathway of knowing — or they may be deceits along a fallacious route of misapprehension and trickery. Understanding may go either way; in a statement like "The stone is green," the word "green" is just as true, or false, as when it is used in a statement like "God's message comes with the renewing green of spring." The moral truth or falsehood of any sentence does not depend on the logic which inheres in words themselves, that is, whether the word "green" is as applicable to stones as to springtime, but on the conditional, the approximate, the ever-unfulfilled degree to which that sentence *means* something true or false to the speaker, the writer, the hearer, or the reader. A sentence, any sentence, is a dimension of reality at the moment of its being known; it is true or false, valid or absurd, because men can experience in words just as truly as they can in life.

One hastens to draw a distinction between this idea of language and the principles of modern neopositivists for whom any statement is true or nonsensical simply because all words are basically self-contradictory. The word "green" of the statement "The stone is green" is nonsense when it is used in a statement like "Her eyes are green": the green of the lady's eyes is a quite different meaning of "green" from that of the stone. Modern logicians make of language an intellectual plaything.[9] Moreover, one must insist that Edwards never employed the logic of the absurd on Scriptural statements; they are, as it were, irrefutable and are not subject to the conditions of normal discourse. Holy Writ allows for logistic and linguistic absurdity only in such patent and rare examples as "The fool hath said in his heart, There is no God." The initial word "fool" at once reduces the statement "There is no God" to nonsense.

Edwards attacked the idea of the *consensus gentium* from still another direction — that of the pleasure-pain argument, the moral-sense assumption that man is a being who finds the good in that which pleases him and evil in that which pains him. Just as in the linguistic argument concerning positive, negative, and neutral, Edwards could ask: Is human choice always moved by the strongest motive? The answer is, of course: It is not, else it would always and uniformly follow those motives which bring it the most good. If, accordingly, the human consciousness does not always choose the strongest motive, it must therefore have choice over the motives which excite it. Thus the will is free to act in accord with or independently of those incentives which beset it.

Edwards showed that simply to choose between a stronger or a weaker motive, a pleasurable or a painful one, necessitates that there be a predisposition to make that choice even before the choice is made: "some tendency to *induce* and dispose to volition," Edwards stated, is "previous to volition itself." [10] He cut the ground from beneath the moral-sense and the Utilitarian thinkers as brilliantly as anyone ever has, for he showed that, if the will has no power to control the causes which bring about the feelings of pleasure or pain, it has no power over the outcome and results. Pleasure and pain are not self-regulatory but inevitable. From sensation to impression, from impression to idea, and from idea to action, the will is powerless.

The Vestiges of Creation. Edwards conducted his argument as though the cloudy evidence of this world gave very little support to the idea of the will. Only occasionally, as in the reference to the telescope,[11] did he use the cogent data of modern science. He should not be charged with anti-intellectualism or with scanting the new learning of his time. To be sure, whenever he needed to deepen and broaden his argument, he took Scripture as his sole authority and, as in Part II, Section 11 of the *Freedom of the Will*, lapsed into the most wearisome series of Biblical analogues. Edwards's use of Holy Writ was not a retreat into a medievalism as if the Cambridge Platonists had never existed; rather, he was seeking for evidence and for a logic of the will apart from the world of simple objects and Newtonian order, neither of which offered the slightest support for — indeed, they even denied — the existence of the will. Edwards well knew that the evidence of the material world in his time in no way supported a concept of the mind: the men of the eighteenth century were suspended over "Descartian vortices" just as truly as was Melville a century later; for, by separating the evidences of the mind's behavior from the immutable activity of the world, Descartes (and Locke and Hume after him) forever disjoined laws of the mind from the laws of nature. The proofs of the mind are cognitive and intellectual, and the defenses of the world are worldly. One should not fall into the error of so many eighteenth-century savants who reasoned from principles and followed arguments wherein not even so much as a first principle can be found. One should not consider atoms as spiritual entities if he can find no evidence of "spirit" in atoms; one cannot reason about motion and space on the moon if he has no idea that measurable space and instants of clocked time exist on the moon.

If Edwards denied that will was somehow functioning within the immutable cause-and-effect world, he thereby reasoned, quite correctly, that the world does not itself possess a will: it nowhere acts on its own initiative. Nor does the world show evidence that a will exists somehow outside that world: will is not imposed from above, for the laws of this world are self-contained and not self-generating. A law does not make itself, nor does it make another law; it did not acquire a will as it functioned from primordial time to the present: acts of nature are no different now from what they ever were. Laws of motion and force are, as Newton suggested, just those discrete laws, or approximations to fundamental rules of the universe, and nothing else.

Edwards's argument was directed largely against the common fallacy that man is the only creature endowed with a will in an otherwise will-less universe. No evidence survives that man could have discovered or been allowed to understand an "Uncreated idea" of will at some stage of his slow emergence from primitive ignorance into knowledge; and just as certainly man could not have received a will or the knowledge of will as a supernatural gift of God. Why should God bestow on man the freedom of the will any more than He would release man from the penalty of suffering and death? Free will could no more have come into existence as a gift of God or as an organic production of nature than a tree can will into existence its roots and branches or desire to extend itself majestically toward heaven.[12]

Nor can an act of will go counter to the laws of nature: man cannot will that the earth cease its rotation; just as certainly man cannot have a volition which is contrary to his own nature: one cannot will that he become something that he is not. Edwards reasoned, as did Hume, that human will is merely another version of the world of substance. Will acts in concert with every pulse, every motion of the universe of matter; any act of volition is forever predisposed to be what it must, for each act, if it is of will, is determined by all acts of the "will of nature" antecedent to it. No human mind can go counter to its own predisposition. "For 'tis absurd," Edwards declared, "to suppose the same individual will oppose itself, in its present act; or the present choice to be opposite to, and resisting present choice: as absurd as it is to talk of two contrary motions, in the same moving body, at the same time. And therefore the very case supposed never admits of any trial, whether in opposing or resisting will can overcome this necessity."[13]

Edwards's reasoning is, to be sure, not irrefutable. It supposes that all acts of willing and doing are "caused" by all acts which precede them; but it disavows any immediate, instantaneous causes by which such prior actions have come into being. They too are caused by an unbroken lineage of precedence and motivation which reach back to some primordial first cause; yet once the logic of causation has been traced backward to that first stimulus, it thereupon takes refuge in mystery by ascribing that original, primal motivation to a single act of divine consciousness which is, however, virtually inexplicable and certainly concealed from the dim understandings of men. If, therefore, the whole route of cause and act is from its beginning a mystery, then surely the single acts of volition and motion are also inexplicable, and man lives in a world which everywhere defies his understanding. One can take refuge in this admission that mystery and confusion lie at the basis of thought and action if one seeks only for a systematic, naturalistic interpretation of the world and of human behavior. Just as Edwards argued, the domain of nature's practical, everyday monotony does not offer much support for a theory of the will or of the mind. He was forced to consider such an argument because his age put such faith in the lineaments and vestiges of creation that to discredit or cast doubt on a simple naturalism of atoms in motion as supporting the existence of the will would seriously undermine a major delusion of the age. There was another and better argument to counter the idea of free will, and Edwards turned to it.

The Moral Reason. Edwards raised not only the empirical and the epistemological but the moral issue as well: What if, in any given situation, a particular act had in fact been performed differently, would the judgment of that act be necessarily and proportionately different? Does the slightest variation in an action incur a proportionate variation in reward or blame? The answer was, logically, of course not. A man who steals a small amount of money and a man who absconds with a vast sum do not receive punishments in precise ratio to the amounts stolen; differing degrees of blame or praise forever confound the judgments of men. Yet, if men were truly endowed with a "moral reason" which, as the moral-sense logicians reasoned, remains unbroken through generations and in spite of darkness and oppression, then the degree of moral judgment should remain constant, and moral laws could correctly affect both criminals and saints.

Suppose, as Edwards reasoned most cogently, an act of the will were a free act; that act would therefore be "rewardable or punishable." The instant the act is rewardable or punishable it ceases to be a free act because it had to be a necessary, an unwilled act in order to be rewarded or punished. A free act supposes, as Edwards said, that "there must be an infinite number of free acts in succession, without any beginning, in an agent that has a beginning." Every free act must therefore be "a necessary effect" in "the whole infinite chain" of cause and effect.[14]

Then the question arises: In such an argument, is there any basis for individual reward and punishment, praise and blame, human good and evil? Edwards's reasoning ended, as it would for Emerson, in proposing that the greatest good is in doing what one knows one has to do in just the way it is done. The most enlightened moral insight is to understand that everything one does, from the flexing of his little finger to the ultimate destiny of his life, has been absolutely and irrevocably foreordained by God's first thought in His universe. Evil is, accordingly, not an act committed, for God cannot allow any deed to go counter to His inviolable logic; evil is God's permission that man may think against or in defiance of the divine will. The sinful thought or the evil deed sets in motion, not a cruel and tormenting sequence of events in the natural order, but a train of tragic dissociation in the sinner himself. Evil is, therefore, a part of the "being" of the evildoer; it is a physical, an emotional, a spiritual removal of the "being" or consciousness — a man's whole nature — from that "consent of being" or harmony of being which God has immutably placed in His universe. The evil man is, by God's prevision, to think and become what Hawthorne would call, in slightly different terms, "the outcast of the universe." Man is threatened with damnation when he becomes convinced that he has a will, that his will acts freely, and that he himself sets in motion a wholly new chain of moral causation every time he thinks or acts.

Man is free when he lives within the restraints of God's moral order; man is enslaved when he presumes to go beyond the boundaries which that order imposes.[15] God is never bound to reward the good and punish the guilty according to their deserving; His judgments are apart from any law of retribution which man may ever conceive. If men convince themselves that they live in a world divinely ordered for their advantage and pleasure and that they can continually recovenant with God the terms of their salvation and success, then they are guilty of the most heinous blasphemy and atheism. Since God exists, then His necessity, His prior will and justice exist; sin and suffering, enlightenment and joy are human responses to a universe of invariable logic and true meaning.

Such a view of evil may condemn the sinner, even when he is unaware that he has sinned, and it may account for places where evil festers in the world; it hardly accounts for the harm that sin does in the world. Are the innocent victims to be soothed by seeing the wicked man glorying in his presumption of sinlessness? Is spiritual blindness an answer to the horror some men bring into the lives of men? Hell, even Edwards's metaphysical and phenomenal hell, is no unction to the hurt and the maimed.

Edwards was concerned with the phenomenology, not the sociology, of evil. To reason why the innocent must suffer for crimes they did not commit was to impute to man a power and judgment he does not possess. God's will had forever construed what would be evil and what would be good: "The sovereignty of God is his ability," Edwards declared, "to do whatever pleases him." [16] The stars in their places, the minute particles of matter in theirs were but manifestations of a law which God had instituted and intended to maintain; the cause and effect of every act throughout all time were foreordained by the very first thought and the very first energy of the primal atom. That evil seemed to be a coefficient of history and that men were born by the millions to be miserable and be doomed was a principle whose secret no man could ever finally penetrate.

Freedom of the Will, for all its dire and forbidding logic, was not wholly an assault on the prevailing notion that man acts from the privilege of choice which nothing else in the universe possesses. The end of the book may be as remorseless as any treatise in human morals, for it leaves man a mere cipher in the cosmos. Edwards's journey from the excitement and the openness of "Of Insects" and "The Mind" to the ironically titled *Freedom of the Will* had been toward limitation and contraction; yet it had been the distance along a line which had curved from the outer universe down to the inmost self. A lifetime follows this line not because it wishes to do so but because it must; the world of substance is not abandoned; rather, the wonder of the will is that it must follow the way it alone can go along the route God has required it to follow every second of its life. It must learn, even as does the mind, its own signs, its own iconography of consciousness. Man's discovery of his littleness and triviality is a way of knowing the world, even as one's being born again is a way to the Kingdom of Heaven; in either case, the growth of one's private mind is man's most valid exercise in understanding and of worship. One can — indeed one must — build a world from within.

Epilogue

EDWARDS was not destined to spend his last years on the edge of the American wilderness, there to inquire into the varieties of human consciousness and the limitations of man's will. In September, 1757, the trustees of New Jersey College, as it was then called, voted to name Edwards to succeed to the presidency which had been held by his son-in-law, Aaron Burr. He accepted and arrived on February 16, 1758, to be formally inducted on that day. One week later he was inoculated for smallpox, and on March 22 he was dead. His grave still honors Princeton University, the institution he was unable to serve.

In his own time Edwards was an anomaly. He seemed to his contemporaries to be the passionate supporter of a body of doctrine and thought which, if not discredited altogether, was at best inappropriate to the times and to the lives men lead in this world. To argue that God had so limited man's will as to make him little more than an atomic cipher in the universe; to declare that the incoming of grace was mysterious and wonderful beyond words, and yet that men who have the experience of salvation never really know they are saved; and to demolish any lingering notions that God stands ever ready to receive the repentant sinner — these positions made Edwards's ministry seem out of place in an age which encouraged the spirit of man to achieve in concert with God, if not the Holy City God had intended, at least some semblance of His way in this world of ever-increasing power and good. Edwards's warnings became more forbidding and then, in 1751, they ceased altogether: thereafter Edwards worked diligently among his parishioners, ministered to the needs of the Indians, and turned in upon himself where his spiritual resources seemed boundless. Isolation and exile were a boon; they allowed Edwards to finish the grand instauration upon which he had embarked in his youth.

Edwards knew and used the insights of his age in their most radical form. The term "radical" is meant literally: he continually traced ideas and their behavior to their beginnings. He had an intellectual historian's passion for roots and causes; thus he be-

146

came a chronicler of the Awakening, not merely as it was a further demonstration of God's ways among men, but as it displayed
in the lives of men and women those effective energies which
determine human character. All those energies were, he knew,
caused and therefore never self-willed. How could there be any
private thought when all seeing and knowing come from the data
of impressions which the universe of fact provides? How can
there be any unique feeling, any personal mood or idea, any singular awareness of God and eternity, if all apprehension is merely
a replica of substance and all ideas conform to the lineaments and
motions of things? And what are words except sounds and shapes
which are not really true but only what the generality of men
have supposed to be true? Edwards took the eighteenth-century
question — Who am I in my own person and knowledge? — and
made it a way into those dark pathways of self-inquiry which the
century had presumably abandoned together with a host of superstitions. He maintained his spiritual and intellectual discipline
in point-for-point relevance with the thought of his age — and he
undercut it at every moment.

In the life of his mind Edwards discovered, sometime in his
middle years, that the glowing wonder of sense perception was
failing him; he could no longer see the world of external objects
and know that inner domain of thought as forever according in
some marvellous way with the ring of wonder God had placed
for man to know. Perhaps Edwards's sense experience weakened;
more likely, Edwards came to understand that the world of objects and forms, however marvellous to the eye and to the mind,
was predetermined from the first atom that moved to the last
action of God in His universe. To insist, as Edwards did from the
early years of his ministry, that God had predetermined His universe was not to deny it any wonder or divinity; indeed, God
could be seen acting in and through it with clarity and necessity.
What the doctrine of God's sovereignty meant for Edwards was
that he turned from the ethical nature of the universe to the
ethical content of immediate, private existence. He became an
analyst of individual experience at a time when most men regarded "experience" as necessarily conforming to the age-old
laws of atoms in motion and the general behavior of humankind.

A man's life is bound, inevitably; but its ethical content — the
quality of his belief and the depth of his faith, the exercises of his
mind and soul — is not bound. Ideas may be developed in strict
accord with a world of causation, but they become thought, they

are formed by a man's character, and they are made a part of his inward content of life. Force, action, matter in motion, the vast coherent design of the universe are all according to law. The human mind, the movement of knowing from sense to thought, the perceptions of the soul are shaped and known as they are a part of character; and character is a man's spiritual estate.

Edwards turned away from things and facts, from sense and delight, from spiders and living objects, and sought instead the secret springs of private being: he may have found them only in the most limited way of the ironically titled *Freedom of the Will*, but he found them nevertheless. "There is nothing like our ideas," he wrote, "existing in the bodies themselves." Our ideas are what we have found for ourselves in the daily, the instant, and in the supremely difficult and glorious ways we live our lives. In the heart and in the soul abides our vision of ourselves, and even our God.

At a time when Puritanism in America had abandoned its sense of man's terrible desolation in the world, Edwards appeared and, in his own life and thought, re-enacted the Puritan drama of the lonely soul. In his twin masterworks of his latter years he made a complete resolution of his Puritan thought and the articulate energy of his own time. In *The Treatise Concerning Religious Affections* he demonstrated that God moves in His world toward man: this was a Puritan argument. In the *Freedom of the Will* he showed how little man is capable of doing on his own beyond realizing his sublime triviality, his littleness of being: this was the devastation Edwards effected when he brought his very considerable logic and imaginative force to bear on the eighteenth-century doctrine that man is free because God gave him his freedom and that the exercise of that freedom redounds to the greater glory of God. Humankind often finds a comfortable place for itself and lives with the conviction that it is every hour meriting the applause of a universe designed only for its special praise and favor. Edwards posed the mind against reality, the unique man against the generality of mankind, and the soul against the dark, enveloping shadow of its own destiny. He himself traced and followed that way, and then he left his testament for others to heed if they chose.

NOTES

1 (pages 1-19). The Inclining World of God

1. Much of the information on Edwards's life in this and succeeding chapters is derived from Ola Elizabeth Winslow, *Jonathan Edwards, 1703-1758: A Biography* (New York, 1940) and Sereno E. Dwight, *The Life of President Edwards* (New York, 1830).

2. This composition Dwight assigned to Edwards's thirteenth year. Edwards wrote two versions of "Of Insects": the first and more complete is printed in the *Andover Review*, XIII (1890), 5-13 (citations in this chapter are to this version); the second is in Dwight, pp. 23-28, written in the form of a letter.

3. The youthful Edwards was well aware of Newton's theory of light. In "Of Insects" he noted that the "Chief Reason" that certain particles suspended in air may be brightened and intensified "must be Referred [to] that incurvation of the Rays Passing by the edge of any body which Sir Isaac Newton has proved." Newton formulated what became known as the corpuscular theory of light. According to this hypothesis, light is to be regarded as a flight of material particles emitted by a source; the sensation of light is therefore produced by the mechanical impact these particles have on the human eye. Newton's principle of "incurvation" stated that particles of light are curved or deflected by objects along the physical pathway of that light; in some of these deflections the particles are absorbed and the light becomes dim; in some the light is relayed with additional intensity and thus strikes the retina with increased physical impact. Newton even recombined the spectrum colors and formed them into white light. He thereby proved that color was not in the glass of the prism and was not produced by the refraction of light rays through a prism which served to add or induce color but that colors were originally present in the white light; the function of the prism was merely to separate or sort them out by deviating rays of different colors through different angles. For Edwards the significance of Newton's theory of optics was that it helped him answer the nagging issue of objects in nature as having mere objectivity and also as having location and meaning in a phenomenological universe.

4. "Of Being" was first printed by Dwight (pp. 706-8) as part of "Notes on Natural Science." A better text is that of E. C. Smyth, "Some Early Writings of Jonathan Edwards," *Proceedings of the American Antiquarian Society*, n.s., X (1895), 237-47.

5. See William Ames, *The Marrow of Sacred Divinity* (London,

149

1638), pp. 32-33: "Hence that beginning in which God is said to create the World, was the end of that duration which nothing had, and the beginning of that which the world had."

6. Dwight (p. 30) dated Edwards's reading of Locke's *Essay* to "the second year of his collegiate course," or 1717. The case for Locke's influence is made by Perry Miller, *Jonathan Edwards* (New York, 1949), pp. 38, 52-67, and by E. H. Davidson, "From Locke to Edwards," *Journal of the History of Ideas*, XXIV (July, 1963), 355-72.

7. "The Mind" or "Notes on the Mind," as it is sometimes titled, has had a strange and baffling history. The first text, transcribed presumably from Edwards's own manuscript, was published by Dwight in an Appendix, pp. 664-702. Thereafter the manuscript disappeared and has never been seen since. Dwight's text was reprinted by E. C. Smyth, pp. 213-36, with differing headings and new arrangement of the paragraphs. A modern though by no means definitive version is that edited by H. G. Townsend, *The Philosophy of Jonathan Edwards from His Private Notebooks* (University of Oregon Press, 1955), pp. 21-73. An interesting argument for restoring the various paragraphs in "The Mind" to their original state has been advanced by Leon Howard, who has supplied an interesting commentary; see *"The Mind" of Jonathan Edwards: A Reconstructed Text* (University of California Press, 1963).

8. Dwight, p. 30.

9. *An Essay Concerning Human Understanding*, ed. Benjamin Rand (Harvard University Press, 1931).

10. *An Essay Concerning Human Understanding*, ed. A. C. Fraser (Oxford, 1894), I, 103.

11. *Ibid.*, p. 113.

12. *Ibid.*, p. 87.

13. *Ibid.*, II, 351.

14. *Ibid.*, I, 170. Cf. Justus Buchler, "Art and Object in Locke," *Philosophical Review*, XLVI (September, 1937), 528-35. For a recent treatment of this problem, see R. W. Chisholm, *Perceiving: A Philosophical Study* (Cornell University Press, 1957), pp. 126-31.

15. Cf. A. N. Whitehead, *Process and Reality: An Essay in Cosmology* (New York, 1929), p. 87.

16. *Essay*, ed. Fraser, I, 371.

17. *Ibid.*, p. 384. For a cogent treatment of Locke's theory of language, see D. J. O'Connor, *John Locke* (London, 1952), pp. 123-52.

18. Townsend, p. 42.

19. *Ibid.*, pp. 25, 23.

2 (pages 20-36). Sovereign God and Reasoning Man

1. Dwight, pp. 68, 69.
2. *The Works of President Edwards,* ed. Sereno E. Dwight (Worcester, Mass., 1808), I, 33. (This edition is hereinafter cited as *Works.*)
3. *Dokumente zu Luthers Entwicklung,* ed. Otto Scheel (Tübingen, 1929), II, 116; see Erik H. Erikson, *Young Man Luther: A Study in Psychoanalysis and History* (New York, 1958), p. 23.
4. *Works,* I, 41.
5. Thomas H. Johnson, "Jonathan Edwards' Background of Reading," *Publications of the Colonial Society of Massachusetts,* XXVIII (1931), 193-222.
6. Dwight, p. 114.
7. *Ibid.,* pp. 114-15.
8. *Ibid.,* pp. 106, 105.
9. *Ibid.,* p. 103.
10. *Ibid.,* pp. 106, 107.
11. Dwight gives the date as July 28 (p. 113), Winslow as July 20 (p. 115).
12. *Works,* VII, 473.
13. *Ibid.,* p. 474.
14. This logic is, as Edwards would come to understand, evasive, if not wrong. When men presumably "see" atom or absolute, cause or effect, substance or idea, they may not be understanding something that is a fact of nature or a picture in the mind; rather, they may be assuming a willed continuity which has no supportable logic. The volitional approach to ideas, as demonstrated by Hume and Edwards, always called in question the principle of causation which Bacon had outlined and which most men in the eighteenth century trusted. Another argument which Edwards learned while he was in college was the attack on causation and substantiality which had been made in the seventeenth century by the group of English religious philosophers known as the Cambridge Platonists, whose writings were well-known in New England. Clergymen and laymen like Samuel Sewall had the writings of Henry More, Benjamin Whichcote, and Ralph Cudworth on their bookshelves; More's *Enchiridion Ethicum* was a textbook at Harvard as late as 1726; and Cudworth's massive and monumental *True Intellectual System of the Universe* (1678) was a work to which Edwards referred quite frequently in his notes and published writings. The large question of the importance of the Cambridge Platonists in the intellectual life of New England was ignored until the study of Emily S. Watts, "Jonathan Edwards and the Cambridge Platonists" (unpublished Ph.D. dissertation, University of Illinois, 1963).

15. *Works*, VII, 469-70.
16. *Ibid.*, pp. 472, 473.
17. *Ibid.*, pp. 480, 481.
18. *Ibid.*, p. 484.

3 (pages 37-56). The Covenant and God's Incentives

1. Edward's own most comprehensive treatment of Original Sin and the two Covenants is *The Great Christian Doctrine of Original Sin Defended*, written toward the end of his life and published in 1758.
2. *Works*, VIII, 233.
3. Increase Mather, *The Doctrine of Divine Providence* (Boston, 1684), p. 7. For an extended treatment of this subject, see Perry Miller, "The Marrow of Puritan Divinity," *Publications of the Colonial Society of Massachusetts*, XXXII (1937), 277-300.
4. *Mather Papers*, VIII, 119-20.
5. *The Compleat Body of Divinity* (Boston, 1702), p. 11.
6. *Ibid.*, p. 151.
7. *The Doctrine of Original Sin*, p. 217.
8. *Seasonable Thoughts on the State of Religion in New-England* (Boston, 1743), p. 207. In his "Observations Concerning Faith" Edwards exposed the fallacy as cleverly as anyone has: "It has ever been counted to be good reasoning from the effect to the cause; and it is a way of reasoning that common sense leads mankind to. But if, from a different effect, there is no arguing any difference in the cause, this way of reasoning must be given up. If there be a difference in the effect, that does not arise from some difference in the cause, then there is something in the effect that proceeds not from its cause, viz. that diversity; because there is no diversity in the cause to answer it: Therefore, that diversity must arise from nothing, and consequently is no effect of anything; which is contrary to the supposition. So this hypothesis is at once reduced to a contradiction . . . and is the same thing as to say, that nothing produces something" (*Works*, IV, 484).
9. *Seasonable Thoughts*, p. 204.
10. David Hume, *A Treatise of Human Nature*: "The mind is a kind of theatre, where several perceptions successively make their appearance; pass, repass, glide away, and mingle in an infinite variety of postures and situations" (I. IV. V.).
11. *Works*, VIII, 294.
12. *Ibid.*, p. 296.
13. *Ibid.*, p. 294.
14. *Ibid.*, pp. 297, 298.
15. *Ibid.*, p. 297.

16. *Ibid.*, VII, 477.
17. Dwight, p. 105.

4 (pages 57-82). The World as History

1. Whitefield first came to America in 1739; the trip of 1740 into New England lacked a little more than a month. He arrived in Boston on September 18, spent ten days there and in the immediate neighborhood, went to Northampton where he remained four days, and then moved south into Connecticut and back to Philadelphia (see Winslow, p. 180). Whitefield was a guest in the Edwards house from Friday, October 17, to the following Monday (*ibid.*, p. 186; see Dwight, p. 146). The most succinct account of this phase of the Awakening is Edwards's letter to the clergymen of Boston, dated December 12, 1743 (Dwight, pp. 160-70).
2. *Treatise Concerning Religious Affections,* ed. John E. Smith (Yale University Press, 1959), p. 138.
3. *Works,* II, 14.
4. *Ibid.*, p. 87.
5. *Ibid.*, pp. 92, 382.
6. *Ibid.*, III, 393.
7. *Ibid.*, p. 392.
8. *Ibid.*, pp. 426-27.
9. This argument is carefully considered in *A Justification by Faith Alone* (*Works,* VII, 124 ff.); it was undertaken later in *The Great Christian Doctrine of Original Sin Defended* (*Works,* VI, 296-301).
10. Edwards saw in his own time the approaching realization of the prophecies of Daniel and the Apocalypse; just before the last hour of the world, the Church of God seems almost to disappear as the power of Satan increases: "Hitherto this prophecy has been very signally fulfilled; since the reformation, the kingdom of Antichrist has been remarkably filled with darkness in this respect" (*Works,* III, 438). Yet, for all his reliance on the immediate truth of the books of Daniel and Revelation, he quibbled over the precise meaning of the mystic numbers seven, ten, seventy, and 144,000, for to accept them as literally true would be to accept the prophecy of the slaying of the witness of the Lord just before the last hour. Edwards's humanity recoiled from this awful prospect: ". . . in the general," he wrote, "Satan and Antichrist shall not get the victory, nor greatly prevail" (p. 449), and he could not accept the precise chronological interpretation of history as set forth by the learned Moses Lowman, *A Paraphrase and Notes on the Revelation of St. John* (London, 1737). Edwards tended to look upon the coming of the last hour as the sweep of God's Word across oceans so that within a century (in man's time) the whole of Mohammedanism and heathendom would be

converted; yet he had to confess, rather sadly, that the prospect was only a dream (see pp. 468-69).

11. See Ames, *Marrow of Sacred Divinity*, pp. 134-41.

12. Edwards was not, however, aware of such a rudimentary linguistic principle that the Scriptures are fusions of varying texts and that, for example, the words *Jehovah* and *Elohim*, while they did designate "God," were names of the deity known respectively to the people of the southern and of the northern kingdoms after the division of the Jews; see *Reasons Against Dr. Watts's Notion of the Pre-existence of Christ's Human Soul* (*Works*, IV, 494).

13. *Works*, III, 9-24.

14. *Ibid.*, p. 53.

15. *Ibid.*, pp. 45, 46, 49, 59.

16. *Ibid.*, pp. 71, 76.

17. *Ibid.*, p. 65.

18. *Ibid.*, VII, 495, 496.

5 (pages 83-103). The World, Faith, and True Virtue

1. *Works*, VII, 9-10.

2. *Ibid.*, pp. 11, 12, 14, 15.

3. *Ibid.*, pp. 17, 22-23.

4. *Ibid.*, pp. 124, 125, 128.

5. *Ibid.*, p. 65.

6. *Ibid.*, II, 397.

7. Edwards always insisted on the derivation of words from a common, "determinate origin": men begin to speak because they must survive; the words they fashion and make into a language are always bound to the necessities of daily living. Yet there is a difference between the eventual meanings of common words and those words "that are used to express such acts of the mind" as, for example, "faith" and "salvation." Their meanings are obscure and "of a very indeterminate signification. It is difficult," Edwards concluded, "to find words to exhibit our own ideas" (*Observations Concerning Faith, Works*, IV, 437).

8. *Ibid.*, II, 396-97.

9. *Ibid.*, pp. 411-12.

10. *Ibid.*, p. 414.

11. See A. Owen Aldridge, "Edwards and Hutcheson," *Harvard Theological Review*, XLIV (January, 1951), 35-53.

12. *Works*, II, 417, 419.

13. *Ibid.*, pp. 424-25.

14. *Ibid.*, p. 440.

15. *Ibid.*, pp. 464-65.

16. *Ibid.*, pp. 469-71.

17. *Ibid.*, VI, 34.

18. *Ibid.*, p. 54.
19. *Ibid.*, p. 14.
20. *Ibid.*, p. 31.
21. *Ibid.*, p. 33.
22. *Ibid.*, pp. 116-17.
23. *Ibid.*, p. 117, 120-21.
24. *Ibid.*, pp. 122, 124.

6 (pages 104-126). Sovereign God and Humbled Man

1. Dwight, p. 276.
2. *Works*, VII, 155, 158.
3. See *Works*, III, 355-494; for Edwards's correspondence with the Scottish clergy, see Dwight, pp. 224-46.
4. Only a shortened version is published in *Works*, III, 499-548. For a full text, see *Memoirs of the Rev. David Brainerd . . . Chiefly Taken from His Own Diary. By Rev. Jonathan Edwards. Now for the First Time Incorporated with the Rest of His Diary, in a Regular Chronological Series*, ed. S. E. Dwight (New Haven, 1822). This work was the most frequently reprinted and widely distributed of all that came from Edwards's hand; see Johnson, *Bibliography of Edwards*, pp. 47-60.
5. *Works*, III, 530.
6. *Ibid.*, pp. 523, 522.
7. *Ibid.*, VII, 302-3.
8. *Ibid.*, III, 534-35, 536.
9. *Images or Shadows of Divine Things*, ed. Perry Miller (Yale University Press, 1948), pp. 58, 59.
10. *Ibid.*, p. 88.
11. *Ibid.*, p. 57.
12. *Ibid.*, p. 88.
13. If it "thereby be intended, that a thing must be known to have a real existence before the person has a clear understanding, idea or apprehension of the thing proposed or objected to his view, . . . then the assertion is not true: for his having a clear idea of something proposed to his understanding, or view, as very beautiful or very odious, as is proposed, does not suppose its reality; that is, it does not presuppose it, though its real existence may perhaps follow from it. But in our way of understanding things in general of all kinds, we first have some understanding or view of the thing in its qualities, before we know its existence" (*Works*, IV, 470). Edwards stated this argument late in life in the *Observations Concerning Faith*, but it had remained unchanged over the years.
14. *Images*, p. 60.
15. *Ibid.*, pp. 65, 66.
16. *Ibid.*, pp. 88-89.

17. *The Poems of Edward Taylor*, ed. Donald E. Stanford, with a Foreword by Louis L. Martz (Yale University Press, 1960), p. 257.
18. *Images*, p. 88.
19. *Ibid.*, p. 93.
20. The *Personal Narrative* was written sometime after January, 1739, for it has that date near the end. It was first printed by Dwight and has been reprinted many times. The text used here is that of the *Works*, I, 31-47.
21. *Ibid.*, pp. 47, 37.
22. *Ibid.*, p. 46.
23. *Ibid.*, pp. 33, 41.
24. *Ibid.*, p. 47.

7 (pages 127-145). The Will and the Mind

1. For the complete narrative of Edwards's controversy with and removal from the Northampton Church, see Dwight, pp. 298-403, and Winslow, pp. 215-67.
2. *Works*, I, 120, 126, 141.
3. *Treatise Concerning Religious Affections*, ed. John E. Smith (Yale University Press, 1959), p. 138. Edwards emphasized that the apparent variety of "operations" is most clearly revealed in Holy Writ: the Bible has meanings quite proper to a time and to a people, and then it may lose those meanings which are differently revealed from the one "occasion of the Scripture." Nevertheless, the eternal truth of Scripture is unassailed. William James, considering the *Treatise* from a different time and a differing point of view, called it an "admirably rich and delicate description" (*Varieties of Religious Experience* [London and New York, 1909], p. 239).
4. *Treatise*, pp. 113-14.
5. See Ernst Cassirer, *The Philosophy of the Enlightenment*, trans. F. C. A. Koelln and J. P. Pettegrove (Princeton University Press, 1951), pp. 52-53.
6. For Hume's argument on this point, see *Dialogues Concerning Natural Religion* (Edinburgh and London, 1793), II, 498-99. The first modern commentator to recognize the importance of this principle was Frederic I. Carpenter, "Radicalism of Jonathan Edwards," *New England Quarterly*, IV (1931), 639-44.
7. For a full treatment of Edwards's adversaries in the controversy on the will, see Paul Ramsey's edition of *Freedom of the Will* (Yale University Press, 1957), pp. 65-118.
8. See *ibid.*, pp. 320-21.
9. See G. E. Moore, *Principia Ethica* (Cambridge University Press, 1903; reprinted, 1954), pp. 1-36; Bertrand Russell, *Our Knowledge of the External World* (Chicago and London, 1914), pp. 211-42;

Gilbert Ryle, *The Concept of Mind* (New York, etc., 1949), pp. 25-82.

10. *Freedom of the Will*, ed. Ramsey, p. 230.

11. *Ibid.*, p. 266.

12. In *The Great Christian Doctrine of Original Sin Defended*, which appeared in 1758, four years after the *Freedom of the Will*, Edwards returned to this argument as a means of attacking a then current treatise sustaining the free will — John Taylor's, *The Scripture-Doctrine of Original Sin Proposed to Free and Candid Examination* (Belfast, 1746). Taylor reasoned that the will was a gift of God to man and that Adam, as our first parent, was privileged to exercise his will even if he brought all humanity to its doom. That first act of will in the Fall extended to humankind the power of willing which, even if it bring dire consequences, is forever man's sacred privilege. Edwards began his argument by considering whether or not Adam's first act of willing were from an antecedent power of choice or from the act of choosing itself: "And with respect to Adam, let us consider how . . . it was not possible he ever should have any such thing as righteousness, by any means at all. In the state wherein God created him, he could have had no such thing as love to God, or any love or benevolence in his heart. For if so, there would have been original righteousness; there would have been *genuine moral rectitude*. . . . But if he were wholly without any such thing as love to God, or any virtuous love, how should he come by virtue? The answer will doubtless be, by act of choice: He must first choose to be virtuous. But what if he did choose to be virtuous? It could not be from love to God, or any virtuous principle, that he chose it; for, by the supposition, he has no such principle in his heart: And if he chooses it without such a principle, still, according to this author, there is no virtue in the choice; for all virtue, he says, is to be resolved into that single principle of love. . . . So that there is no way that can possibly be devised in consistence with Dr. Taylor's scheme, in which Adam ever could have any righteousness, or could ever obtain any principle of virtue, or perform any one virtuous act" (*Works*, VI, 263, 264). Edwards's deduction was the one he posed in *Freedom of the Will*: "This is the general notion, not that principles derive their goodness from actions, but that actions derive their goodness from the principles whence they proceed; and so that the act of choosing that which is good, is no further virtuous than it proceeds from a good principle, or virtuous disposition of the mind" (*ibid.*, pp. 259-60).

13. *Freedom of the Will*, p. 159.

14. *Ibid.*, p. 236.

15. Edwards approvingly quoted Locke's *Essay*: "Is it worth the name of freedom, to be at liberty to play the fool, and draw shame and

misery upon a man's self? If to break loose from the conduct of reason, and to want that restraint of examination and judgment that keeps us from doing or choosing the worst, be liberty, true liberty, mad men and fools are the only free men" (*Freedom of the Will*, p. 379n.; cf. *Essay*, ed. Fraser, I, 347).

16. *Freedom of the Will*, p. 378.

INDEX